Catch THE Wave

is a gift to you from

Adventures in Missions

Books by Kevin Johnson

Early Teen Devotionals

Can I Be a Christian Without Being Weird?

Could Someone Wake Me Up Before I Drool on the Desk?

Does Anybody Know What Planet My Parents Are From?

So Who Says I Have to Act My Age?

Who Should I Listen To?

Why Can't My Life Be a Summer Vacation?

Why Is God Looking for Friends?

Books for Teens

Catch the Wave!

Look Who's Toast Now!

What's With the Dudes at the Door?*

For a *Catch the Wave!* study guide and youth missions trip curriculum—or to find out more about Kevin Johnson's books—visit his Web site: http://www.thewave.org

*with James White

Catch the Wave

Kevin Johnson

BETHANY HOUSE PUBLISHERS
MINNEAPOLIS, MINNESOTA 55438

Catch the Wave
Copyright © 1996
Kevin Walter Johnson

Cover design by Terry Dugan.

Jet-Ski Watercraft is a registered trademark of Kawasaki.

Cheez Whiz is a trademark of Kraft Foods.

Mountain Dew is a registered trademark of Pepsico.

Frisbee is a registered trademark of Whammo.

All scripture quotations, unless indicated, are taken from the HOLY BIBLE, NEW INTERNATIONAL VERSION®. Copyright © 1973, 1978, 1984 by International Bible Society. Used by permission of Zondervan Publishing House. All rights reserved. The "NIV" and "New International Version" trademarks are registered in the United States Patent and Trademark Office by International Bible Society. Use of either trademark requires the permission of International Bible Society.

Verses marked TLB are taken from the Living Bible © 1971 owned by assignment by Illinois Regional Bank N.A. (as trustee). Used by permission of Tyndale House Publishers, Inc. Wheaton, IL 60189. All rights reserved.

Verses marked NCV are taken from the New Century Version.

Published by Bethany House Publishers
A Ministry of Bethany Fellowship, Inc.
11300 Hampshire Avenue South
Minneapolis, Minnesota 55438

Printed in the United States of America by
Bethany Press International, Minneapolis, Minnesota 55438

Library of Congress Cataloging-in-Publication Data

Johnson, Kevin W., 1964–
    Catch the wave / Kevin W. Johnson
      p. cm.
    ISBN 1–55661–808–5
    1. Youth—Religious life. 2. Vocation—Juvenile literature.
I. Title.
BV4531.2.J59   1996
248.8'3—dc20
                                             96–25209
                                               CIP

To Elise

You belong to Jesus

KEVIN JOHNSON is Vice President of Training and Resources for Family Hope Services, an agency serving at-risk youth and families in the greater Minneapolis area. He also served as senior editor for adult nonfiction at Bethany House Publishers and pastored a cool group of more than 400 sixth through ninth graders at Elmbrook Church in metro Milwaukee. While his training includes an M.Div. from Fuller Theological Seminary and a B.A. in English and Print Journalism from the University of Wisconsin–River Falls, his current interests include cycling, guitar, and short-wave radio. Kevin and his wife, Lyn, live in Minnesota with their three children—Nate, Karin, and Elise.

Contents

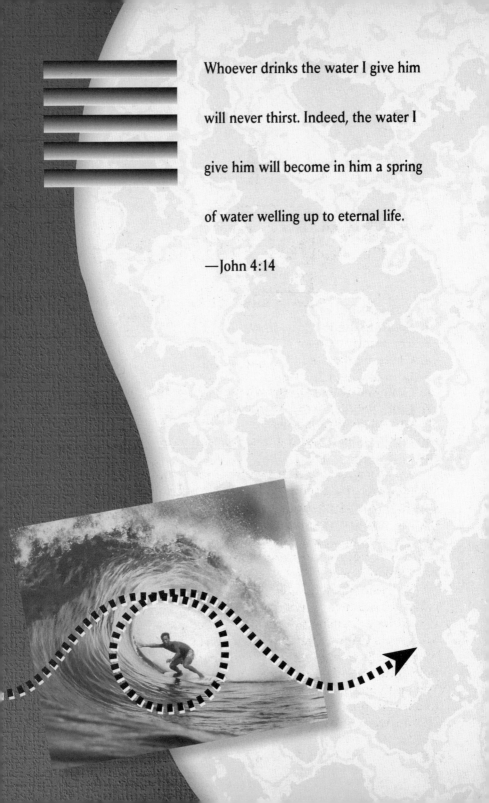

Whoever drinks the water I give him will never thirst. Indeed, the water I give him will become in him a spring of water welling up to eternal life.

—John 4:14

1

A Cool Kind of Dream

From a distance you see what looks like the flash of sun on snow. *Snow? In June?* You have to get close—you almost step in whatever it is—before you realize what covers the ground. Diapers. *Used* diapers. All around your *home away from home*.

A day earlier you'd driven from the United States into Canada with five friends and a couple of adults. Your road trip took you north from Grand Portage—the town at the tip of northeastern Minnesota—eight hours into Ontario. More hours in the truck that morning—off-pavement, jolting down potholed gravel roads—had brought you to Frenchman's Head, a town on a Canadian Indian reserve.

The residents who greet you are quick to share a bit of colorful local history with you. The town, they whisper, is named for a French trader who explored the area two hundred years before. They offer to take you to the spot where the poor Frenchman's head was lopped off and slung on a pole. You hope they're joking. You worry that they're not. You and your friends, they point out, are the first outsiders to dare sleep in the village since.

You were already a little carsick from your trip. Now

you're a little scared. You excuse yourself and step carefully through the diapers to a small battered cabin—your home for the next two weeks. From the front step you look back at the arc of diaper white littering the ground. You can almost see the former mama of the house cracking open the door in the middle of a frozen Canadian winter and launching a diaper across the yard.

You push open the door, not sure you're ready for what's ahead.

You've dreamed for months about Frenchman's Head. When your adult trip leaders talked about your summertime destination you pictured the remote yet posh fishing spots you'd seen in tourist brochures. The diapers, you find, are only a start. The images in your head were all rudely wrong: *Cozy place*—actually a village of 100 people, all but a handful unemployed and bored out of their brains. *Festive atmosphere*—more like nonstop, wall-to-wall drunken brawl. *Starry northwoods nights*—yours to enjoy until they're shattered by a shotgun blast as a wife chases her husband from the house. *Nestled on a pristine lake*—pretty but polluted by human waste leaching from outhouses and infested with microscopic ferbies that melt your intestines. *Panoramic views*—from your own not-so-private doorless outhouse overlooking that lake. *Abundant wildlife*—and the mosquitoes are even bigger than the moose. *An adventure off the beaten path*—as in a half-mile from the far edge of the planet, with summer access by a dirt road cut through the woods just three years ago and winter trips in and out only by ski plane or snowmobile. *Rustic*—no running water, no electricity, no phones.

For two weeks you drink lake water that reeks of the bleach you add to make it sort-of fit to drink. You live on fish and fried bread and peanut butter, sleep on a cold wood floor, and swim and scrub in a lake that thawed about three weeks before—the same place you fill your pails for drinking water.

A romp on the beach it ain't.

So why spend your summer vacation in a place like Frenchman's Head?

Because God is there.

Lifedreams and Sand Castles

Scene change. Back to your world as you know it, week-in after week-out.

You and your friends are sitting in class and the teacher's lecture gets so slow it's like a phone call you can put down and come back to three days later—and not miss anything. Your minds drift off. Quiz time: What do four out of five teenagers dream about?

Okay. *Besides* finding a date for the weekend.

Or maybe here's a better question: What are they *reeeeally* dreaming about?

Hint: Human beings are like big pots of stew. Lots of stuff boils on the surface—weekend plans, homework that's due, spats with friends, job schedules. But if you dig down deep you find out what we're really made of—the goals, hopes, dreams, and desires that fill you and everyone else. It's what's brewing at the bottom of the pot that makes stew what it is.

It's a safe bet that what you and your friends are really pondering is this: a way to be happy. You're dreaming of a good place. A better way. A road map to paradise. A stairway to heaven. Deep down you're thinking about how to capture the flittering bluebird of happiness and wring its little neck until it sings your song.

Everyone wonders what makes life work, what makes it worthwhile. In ten words or less: You ponder what will bring you total, permanent ecstasy. Everyone around you—teen, kid, or adult—wants to find what makes life sizzle. Or at least satisfy.

You have your own ideas of what makes life best. And you don't have to look at your peers for long to see a variety of what they think works:

➥ *The Wealthy Ones.* Money may not buy happiness, but Blake at least seems to have scraped together a good down payment. He plays, dresses, and drives like money is delivered by truck to his house at least once a week. He basks in so much stuff he doesn't know what else to buy. You wish he would buy your school and shut it down.

11

- *The Ultratalenteds.* Tasha has gifts and abilities way beyond normal. She gets voted "Most Likely to Become a Supermodel." Or a chart-busting musician. Or an Olympic gymnast—tough but sleek. Or a ski jumper who defies the odds that she'll end up a smear in the snow.

- *The SafetyFreaks.* Katie won't try anything that might make her a failure or a fool. She's one of the vast crowd of "normal" teens who plays it safe at all costs. She gets Bs, plays sports, sings in the choir, flips burgers after school. Nothing wrong with that. Except it's boring.

- *The Speeders.* David does drugs. Drinks. And gangs, gambling, girlfriends—anything to be able to say, "Wahoo! I feel *good!*" at least three times a day. Anyone can see he has problems. He's headed for a crash and burn. But in the meantime he gets high faster than you can say, "Are you sure that's a good idea?"

- *The Mindmelders.* Emma finds deep meaning by exploring alternative realities. She contacts dead relatives and the sumu wrestlers of ancient Egypt. She entertains extraterrestrials, stuffs voodoo dolls to make her enemies' heads spontaneously combust, and chews mind-twisting fungi.

- *The Resisters.* Marc manages to make a god out of having no God. He thinks the world would be a better place if God just got out of the way.

- *The Brainiacs.* You don't need an example. She's the one who scored better than you on that math test yesterday.

- *The Dropouts.* The nameless, faceless guy who would catch the bus of life to somewhere exciting if he could just find the bus stop.

- *The Policywonks.* Natalie swears that student government actually affects how school runs. She thinks one sweep of her legislative pen would end hunger, stop wars, and put C-SPAN on every TV.

- *The Realists.* Sammy doesn't dream big anymore. He just wants life's bumps paved over, for things to go better. He would settle for friends who don't trash him, a passing grade on his next English test, a face that doesn't make others gag. He wants parents who like each other and who stay sober long enough to pay the rent and buy him some shoes.

➤ *The None-of-the-Aboves*. Kiki is an individual. Proud of it. She's simultaneously retro and avant garde. She doesn't like labels. Shrugs off all of the above. Strange, though—she looks a lot like the other None-of-the-Aboves.

We're all trying to find a way to get by and get happy.

Whether you know it or not, you have a "lifedream." It's the path you're taking with your life—good or bad, crazed or lazy, got-it or just-want-it, chase-it-hard or just-let-it-happen. A lifedream is what you're spending your life trying to achieve.

You don't pick a lifedream thinking it will mess you up. But the wrong dreams are like sand castles. They dissolve into nothingness when a wave washes ashore. The shape or the size isn't what makes it fall. It's the fault of the stuff the castle is made of. It turns out that even the dreams that look sturdy—the least harmful or the most likely to succeed—are at best second best and at worst doomed to fall.

You probably haven't settled on your lifedream—what you want out of life—by sitting down, exploring options, weighing opportunities, and carefully choosing. You don't fire up a computer and play *SimMyLife*.

But what if you *had to* choose? Imagine you're king or queen for the day. What you wish for yourself and your world is what happens. What lifedream would you pick? What approach works? What makes life make sense? What rolls together excitement, friendship, hope, and satisfaction?

You know you're not a queen. Or a king. A long time ago you learned that wishes don't always come true. The gift you hoped for wasn't always waiting for you under the Christmas tree. Friends you trusted messed you up. Sometimes even the parents you believed in weren't around when you needed them most.

But what if you *could* choose? If your wish *would* come true?

Lots of adults say anyone under 30 would only choose a life stuffed with Jet-Skis, brewskis, and big screen TVs. Petty stuff.

Most teenagers—most people, in fact—want more. You want to do what counts, for your life to matter. You might misjudge, though, exactly *what* matters. When you don't know where to find what's best it's easy to gorge your appetites on a lifedream that won't survive or satisfy. Even when you make pretty good choices you still may not grasp what matters most of all.

You might not think to choose God.

God is bigger than anything else imaginable. He is Ultimate Power, Ultimate Intelligence, Ultimate Justice, and Ultimate Love. God burst into history in the person of Jesus Christ to wrap you and your world in total care, total wisdom, total fairness, and total belonging. He wants you to know him. And he wants to make you part of his plan for the world.

A dream is only real if someone is big enough to make the dream come true. Here's God's promise: "Whoever drinks the water I give him will never thirst. Indeed, the water I give him will become in him a spring of water welling up to eternal life" (John 4:14). Jesus says that total satisfaction flows from a relationship with himself. The lifedream he offers is a relationship with himself. Membership in his family.

It's a lifedream with life at its core. It's a lifedream bigger than your wildest dreams. When knowing God well and sticking close to him is the goal of your life, you've found the *real* lifedream. It works and satisfies forever.

You *can* choose what's most important. You *can* choose the lifedream that works. The one that's true and right. And you can be a part of spreading the dream.

Ripples on the Shore

Back to Frenchman's Head.

You spend two weeks playing volleyball, sharing hot dogs, teaching kids Bible lessons and Jesus songs. You teach from "wordless books" that use colored pages to tell a simple message of God's plan for the planet. You hold meetings in the evening and sing. You share stories with the few people in the village willing to come hear you.

After two weeks you leave. You've seen so much drunkenness that you don't ever want to smell alcohol again. You're glad your backside isn't full of buckshot.

You wonder if you did anyone any good.

Your group takes a different road on the way home. For the first time you're able to look across the lake to see the village where you spent the last two weeks. You can't explain it, but you've already seen what you've never seen. You recognize a scene that flashed into your head a few weeks before—a week before you'd even stepped foot in Canada. You were praying for Frenchman's Head. The lake, the hills, the lay of the land—you'd seen the village in your mind when you were praying. Horses and armies battled over the land, like good and evil at war. Unexplainable. Miraculous. Never happened to you before or since.

Still, you return home sure that nothing much had happened.

Until two months later. Two missionaries move to Frenchman's Head for an extended stay. Within a few months a third of the village decides that the God you and your friends talked about was real. They choose a new life-dream. They begin to follow Christ.

You had a part in it.

Cool.

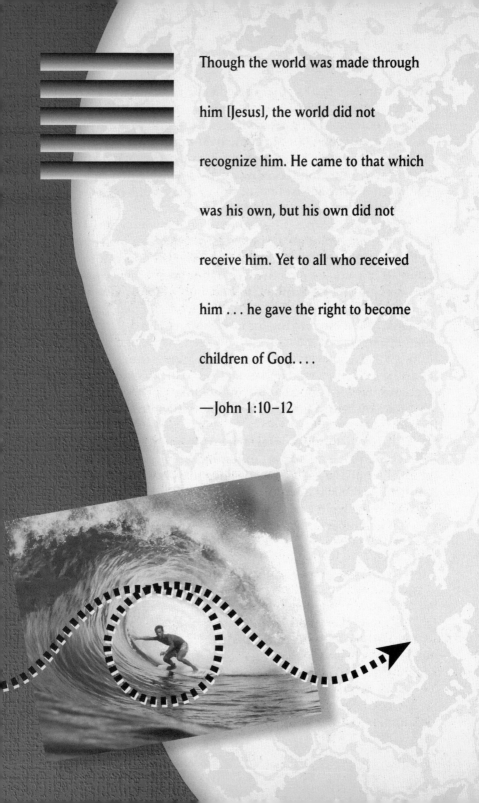

Though the world was made through him [Jesus], the world did not recognize him. He came to that which was his own, but his own did not receive him. Yet to all who received him . . . he gave the right to become children of God. . . .

—John 1:10–12

2

Spotting the
Worldwide Wave

"Skyboarding," says Jack Swain in a flash of brilliance. "We'll make Jesus do a world-record skyboard jump. But picture this"—Swain pauses for effect—"Jesus jumps with no chute. Freefall from 10,000 feet. Lands in a stadium. And he lives."

Swain pounds his fist on the table in front of him. "Can't you see it?" he cries. He turns to Judas, a follower of Jesus. "So can he do it?"

"Yeah. He could do that," Judas vows. "And more. He could go on late-night TV and do some stupid pet tricks. He could turn a hedgehog into a hippopotamus."

"Then, Judas, we have a deal," Swain laughs. "You get this Jesus guy to us and we'll book him all over the country. We'll make him big. Really big."

Talk show hosts had been fighting to get Jesus on their shows. Radio call-in hosts debated whether he was for real. Judas thinks he can make stardom easy for Jesus and make a few bucks for himself. He signs Jesus with the swankest New York promoters he can find.

A week later Jesus quietly wanders off when Judas isn't looking. He doesn't show up for his scheduled skyboardentry stadium gig. At the airport where Jesus is supposed to board his flight to fame, Swain isn't happy. "This is bad, Judas," he stomps. "Very bad. I'm gonna sue you and your mother both. No—I'll take you up in the plane and shove you out myself. You do the jump!"

Judas gets ugly. "It's not my problem. Jesus has a mind of his own. He—"

At the stadium a capacity crowd squints into the sky, seeing nothing. TV announcers broadcasting live across the country struggle to fill dead air. "It seems Jesus is a no-show, a fraud," one snarls. "We're getting reports that Jesus is on the south side of the city—talking with some children, of all things. Let's cut to the studio for comments from callers critical of Jesus. Hello? Long Island, you're on the air. . . ."

The All-Out Jesus Media Blitz (That Never Happened)

What would Jesus look like if he came to the world today?

You wouldn't expect him to be born in a stable or grow up to be a carpenter—a sweaty construction worker. If we had our way, we'd remake Jesus into a president, a movie star, and a superathlete rolled into one.

He'd only sweat with his personal trainer. He'd ditch the beard. He'd need makeup, hair that doesn't flinch in a tornado, and antiperspirant strong enough to keep a gorilla dry under stage lights. And he'd wear sandals only where it was environmentally correct—in the Pacific Northwest (up in the mountains) and in small pockets of enviro-hip Los Angeles.

He'd get wired with a little speaker in his ear so his handlers could tell him what to say. When he spoke he'd have no awkward moments, no lapses in smoothness. He'd offend no one.

He'd stay out of small towns and away from children. The only stops on his world tour would be 60,000-seat stadiums in cities bigger than a million people. When he went out in public he'd be surrounded by bodyguards with antennas in their hats and Uzi burp guns under their suitcoats.

And if everything was planned just right Jesus would be on TV no matter where you flipped. A billion-dollar ad blitz and a swarm of reporters tracking Jesus could make him seem omnipresent—like he was everywhere all the time.

Those are the things that wow us. They get our attention.

Changing the Game

If we had our way, Jesus would be hip and trendy.

But Jesus blows aside our expectations. Even two thousand years ago he refused to play to the crowd just to score first in popularity polls. He came on his own terms.

The facts are these: Jesus gave up the splendor of heaven and was born as a helpless baby (Luke 2:12; Philippians 2:6, 7). He made friends with outcasts and sinners (Matthew 9:10–14). He hung out with children (Luke 18:16). He went to out-of-the-way, dangerous places (John 4:4ff). He showed weakness and cried (John 11:35). He refused to wield power to serve himself (Matthew 26:53). He came as a servant (Matthew 20:28). He forgave his enemies (Luke 23:34). He sweat blood in grief (Luke 22:44). He died an agonizing death on a cross (John 19:17–18).

But *why*? What good did it do for Jesus to act like that?

Jesus' goal was to show us God. Not a god manufactured by a media blowout, but THE REAL GOD.

Jesus didn't just look *like* God. He *is* God. So when Jesus came to earth he showed once and for all what God is like: Jesus "became a human and lived among us. We saw his glory—the glory that belongs to the only Son of the Father— and he was full of grace and truth" (John 1:14, NCV). In Jesus we see "glory"—a shining, completely accurate glimpse of a kind and powerful God. But it isn't quite what we expected.

Jesus didn't come to show off like a model strutting up and down a runway. He had a second goal: to change the world.

A Purpose That Won't Die

Jesus said he came to "seek and to save what was lost" (Luke 19:10). He wasn't talking about searching out lost car keys or misplaced homework. His goal wasn't to locate the remote control stuck in the sofa cushions—though that would be helpful.

He came to help lost *people*. Messed-up human beings. He came to all of us. Jesus came not just to *show* us God the Father but to *bring us back* to the Father.

Here's why: Whenever we disobey what God says is right—whenever we chase a lifedream that isn't centered on God—we get lost. Separated from God.

The truth is that we wandered off. All of us. Now God could have said, "Have it your way! Stay away!" Our disobedience—our sin—deserves the punishment of living forever far from God's presence. (Why do you think they call it "hell"?) Our disobedience earns us permanent separation from God and every good thing—a total, terrifying loneliness on the other side of death.

But God grieved that his friendship with his creation had been broken. Jesus came to open a way—*the one way*—for human beings to become friends with God again. He died on a cross, taking the punishment we deserve.

Some didn't believe who Jesus was, but some did: Jesus "was in the world, and the world was made through him, but the world did not know him. He came to the world that was his own, but his own people did not accept him. But some people did accept him. They believed in him. To them he gave the right to become children of God" (John 1:10–12, NCV). God gives *us* the opportunity to accept Christ *now*—to recognize him as Savior, respecting him as Lord and counting *his* death as *our* death for sin.

When we "receive Christ" we receive God's free gifts: Forgiveness. Membership in God's family. A new lifedream—a life close to your Lord. That's the package the Bible calls "salvation." We're saved from the penalty and the power of sin.

You probably know that. If you're not clear on what it

means to be a Christian, flip ahead and read chapter 10, especially the parts about the "Facts of Life." Don't skip that if you're not sure!

There's more. Jesus didn't stay on the cross. He rose from the grave. He appeared a dozen times to a total of some six hundred people. Forty days after he rose he "ascended" to heaven, shot into the sky, and returned to his Father. Yet when he disappeared into the clouds he didn't say, "Show's over! Fun while it lasted! Go back to normal! Forget I was here!" Jesus didn't rip into history and then roll the closing credits like Porky Pig: "That's all, folks!"

So here's the point of this book: *God's activity on Planet Earth didn't stop when Jesus died on the cross. And he wants you to find your place in his plan to change the world!*

Life Does Go On

So would you recognize Jesus if you saw him today?

You'd have to know what to look for.

If a friend set you up to meet a blind date at the mall you'd get details. You'd want to know time, place, height, weight, hair color, whatever—oh yeah, at least a first name. Then you'd look for a match to the description. You wouldn't mistake as your date the senior citizen handing out cheese samples. Or the pollster holding a clipboard and asking your feelings about male-pattern baldness. You'd know to stay away from anyone who showed up with an open car trunk, a rope, and a chainsaw.

You'll miss what God is doing in your world if you think that anything worth your attention comes wrapped in bright lights, shiny tights, and sound bites. If you want to spot God in action *today* you have to know what to look for. It's the same stuff that was happening when Jesus walked the earth:

1. People **HEAR** about Jesus—they find out that he died on the cross and rose from the dead for them.
2. People **RECEIVE** Jesus—they recognize God as the rightful ruler of the universe, admitting their re-

bellion, accepting God's forgiveness.

3. People **FOLLOW** Jesus—they leave behind wrong dreams and learn to live right.

God didn't die back in the Bible. He's working here, there, and everywhere—all over the planet. People are still HEARING, RECEIVING, and FOLLOWING Jesus:

- Here's a headtwister. It's estimated that around the world 178,000 people became Christians each day in 1994. That's almost 50 per minute—*every* minute— or 65,000,000 for the year! (*Strategic Resources in Run With the Vision, p. 65*). We need an electronic sign— bigger than the lottery kind—to remind us what God is doing.

- In just five short years the number of Christians in Mongolia (the land-locked country to the north of the People's Republic of China) has grown from a tiny handful to as many as 7,000. Many are teenaged girls (*Global Glimpse*).

- In September 1995 an estimated 2.5 *million* students from the United States and around the world gathered at their schools' flagpoles to pray for their schools—the largest youth prayer event in world history. Students who participated in *See You at the Pole* didn't stop there. Many have started Bible clubs and prayer groups and joined to tell non-Christian friends about Christ. (*National Network of Youth Ministries*)

- Kawuri, a new Christian in Nigeria, was tortured by his tribe for his new beliefs. Close to death, he prayed aloud for God to forgive his attackers. Unknown to him, they overheard his prayer. The following night, two Muslim leaders had visions. One saw Jesus, who revealed to him his sins—sins unknown to anyone. The following day both leaders became Christians and took 80 followers to church (*Global Glimpse*).

- Before 1991 there were no churches in Albania, a former stronghold of communism in southern Europe.

Within five years, more than 80 churches had been started and nearly 10,000 people have decided to follow Christ. Albanians are beginning to lead churches and be sent out as missionaries inside and outside of Albania (*Lieds*).

- In many German churches fewer people sit in the pews than sing in the choir. Yet adults are amazed to see God at work among teens. One weekly youth meeting in Frankfurt has burst the walls of one church and moved to a massive Gothic cathedral (*Christianity Today, April 8, 1996, p. 100*).

- A single summer team of teenagers told nearly 19,000 people in Micronesia about Christ—and saw more than 3,200 become Christians (*Teen Missions International, Summer Highlights 1995*).

- In October 1995 at least 30 million Christians in 166 countries participated in the largest prayer event in history. They "prayed through the 10/40 Window," asking God to make himself real to the people of 100 key "Gateway" cities around the world. More than a million churches took part (*AD2000 & Beyond*).

- More than three million people in India saw *Jesus*—a full-length movie based on the book of Luke—in a recent seven-month period. More than 300,000 said they wanted to know more about becoming Christians and more than 700 million people worldwide have seen the film. Have you? (*Global Glimpse* and *Joshua Project 2000*).

What God is doing right now is crashing in all over the world like a mammoth wave. And *The Wave* is too cool to let it wash to shore unnoticed. If you're a teenager in the United States or Canada or a few other places in the world, though, you might have a hard time believing that.

I Don't Get It

Here's the problem: You can't buy a surfboard where the surf seems small. You might not even know enough to feel ripped off. If all you knew about waves was what you spotted in a land-locked muckhole on a dead-still August day you wouldn't want a board anyway.

Until you went to southern California. Or Maui. Or Australia. And saw real waves and world-class surfers.

You might live in a place where the water seems pretty calm. North Americans, for example, make up a mere 15% of the world's Christians. In other words, there are miles of wave-washed coastline you may not even know exist.

Many of us wouldn't recognize a wave if it splashed us in the face. We don't see what God is doing here, there, and everywhere. But if you're willing to look, you'll see *The Wave* crashing in all around you. After all, it's what God has been up to since the beginning of history. . . .

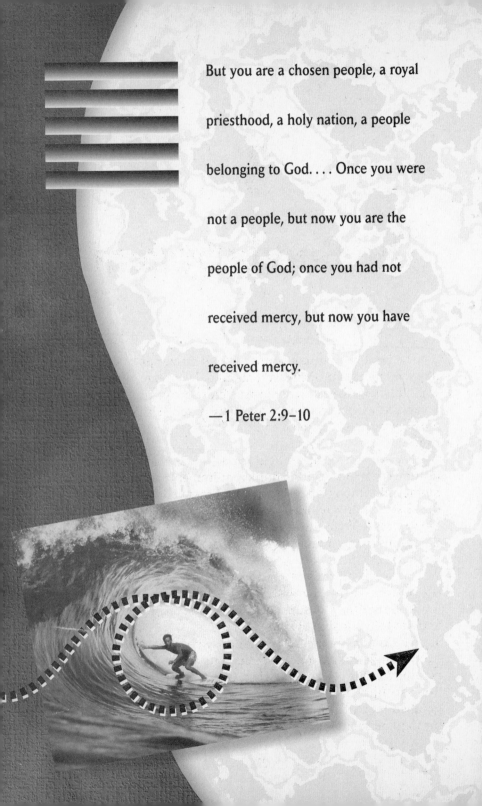

But you are a chosen people, a royal priesthood, a holy nation, a people belonging to God. . . . Once you were not a people, but now you are the people of God; once you had not received mercy, but now you have received mercy.

—1 Peter 2:9–10

3

The Buddy System

The knot in Neesha's stomach spun tighter until she felt like screaming. But she wasn't about to let anyone think she was a pathetic little kid, homesick before she even left home. So as a schoolbus packed with Neesha and her classmates took her away she faked a smile for her mom, who watched from the curb.

It was just a weekend field trip to an environmental education center—a do-it-or-flunk requirement for sophomore biology. But thoughts of the trip had terrified Neesha since the first day of school when she walked into a wall in biology class—35 hostile faces. Everyone huddled in their little groups. For a moment they stared at Neesha. Then they ignored her.

The weekend arrived and the teachers purposely busted up cliques when they assigned cabins. Neesha suddenly found herself in a group of six girls who *had* to get along and *had* to work side by side.

That first evening the big group went on a semi-scary trot through dark woods. Neesha and her five cabinmates became instant teammates when they got lost and took an hour to find their way home. The next morning they groaned together through an obstacle course. They cranked through all their assignments early.

On the bus home Neesha sat thinking quietly. She'd dreaded being alone. But now she had five new friends.

Ice Cream Cones on Hot Cement

People make you shout with glee. And scream in agony. They make you feel liked or hated, supported or abandoned, encouraged or mocked, counted in or left out. It happens wherever you go—school, home, work, church, out and about.

Neesha might head back to school and live happily ever after with her newfound friends. But there's a bigger chance she'll watch those friendships evaporate like an ice cream cone dropped on a hot summer sidewalk. It melts into goo, gets stepped in, sticks to shoes. Then it's gone, licked up by ants and dogs and washed away by the rain. Like it was never there.

Neesha isn't the only one who's uptight about friends. *Relationships drive you.* You want to be liked. You need to feel noticed. You'd ask for a ride—but what if they jabbed the power door locks and sped away? You'd go out for cheerleading or basketball or whatever—but you don't want your friends to think you're stupid. You used to run away from the opposite sex. Now you chase them. And whoda thunk it: You get ill over them.

Relationships protect you. They're why you scurry to compare schedules on the first day of school. They're why you scan the lunchroom for welcoming faces and would sooner go hungry than sit alone. You want friends close by.

That's actually the good news.

There's also bad news. *Relationships can destroy you.* You probably can think of neighbors your age who were your best childhood friends. You grew up. Grew apart. Now you hate each other's guts. Or you might come from a family that's split up—or barely hanging together, like a pane of shattered glass waiting to fall from the frame. Or you've started to fall in love and given away your heart. Then *stomp stomp stomp.* Need more examples of ruined relationships? Probably not.

Adults may laugh off your pained feelings as "adolescent" or "immature." They may psychoanalyze your insecurities. Or they may lecture you about peer fear. But if you worry about how you get along with your friends, your enemies, and everyone in between, there's truth at the core of what you feel. You've caught what's really significant in life. True, you'll wreck your life if you let people run you. But friends—from peers to parents and teachers to God himself—are more important than anything else in the world. Relationships are at the heart of the universe God designed.

Don't Miss This

Plenty of people grotesquely misread the main meaning of the Bible. They warp the truth about what it means to be a Christian. They think that when you follow Jesus you

- *Give up fun.* You follow stupid rules. (It's true that the Bible contains *do*'s and *don't*s. But they're meant to guide us into the best way to live.)
- *Fork over your brain.* You need a lobotomy to believe the Bible. (Check out the book and video series *Don't Check Your Brains at the Door* by Josh McDowell and Bob Hostetler if you wonder about this lie.)
- *Get ugly and intolerant.* You're a narrow-minded person who shoves your ideas on others. (Notice that the people who say this about Christians are usually the ones trying to force others to conform.)
- *Turn weak and huggy kissy.* You use your faith as a crutch to hobble through life. (If you accept what the Bible teaches, you *do* give your life to God and depend on him. But what you tap in to is his unbeatable strength and power.)

The Bible isn't a book of rules or rituals. God doesn't want to manufacture narrow-minded, boring dimdongs. Here's his real goal: He's making a people. One whose hearts belong totally to him. Again and again he says in the Bible, "You will be my people and I will be your God." Read it again in plain English: *The God of the Universe wants to be your friend—and to be friends with the whole planet of other people he created.*

Okay. "Friend" maybe isn't quite the right word—not in the sense of God being your chum, a pal, or buddy, someone you stuff in a pocket and tote around. God *Is* King Over All. He expects not just your affection but your obedience. But you probably think of a king as a stiff old guy in a cape and a crown who liveth in yon royal walled-off castle.

God is way bigger than that. He's also way closer to you than that.

God's whole reason for bringing earth into existence is for us to have real relationships with himself and with each other. That, in fact, is *The Wave* crashing in all over the world:

Big Swell Truth #1

The Wave is God's plan to build a tight group of friends who belong to him— friends who honor him as their master and rely on his care now and forever.

God is building those relationships *right now* as people hear the message of Christ, receive Christ and his forgiveness, and follow Christ—living God's way. But *The Wave* is also what God has been up to *all along*.

If you've been sitting in Sunday school since you were little you may never have thought of the Bible as anything more than a string of unrelated do-good stories. You might not have recognized that the Bible is really a record of how God has been working his plan from the beginning of time. This is the Bible's big picture, the theme you can spot from beginning to end—in seven high and low points in the history of the universe:

The Friendship Stage (Genesis 1–2)

The first small chunk of the Bible shows Adam and Eve in the Garden of Eden enjoying an unspoiled relationship with God. God walks in paradise and talks with Adam and Eve. People aren't God's small-brained pets. They're his hand-picked friends. There were no lies, no tricks, no secrets between the first husband and wife. No clothes—nothing to hide. No deodorant—nothing stunk.

The world worked the way God meant it to work. Everyone got along.

The Fallout Stage (Genesis 3–11)

It didn't take long for the human race to become like a friend who goes psycho on you in a one-sided fight—you do nothing wrong, but suddenly she or he hates you. God did everything right, but Adam and Eve stopped believing he loved them. They stopped trusting that he knew and wanted what was best for them. For the first time the first couple of the world fought with God and clobbered each other. They sinned.

The result? They shattered the friendship they had with God. What began in perfection ended in defection—Adam and Eve were barred from God's presence in the paradise. And they passed on their imperfection. When they had kids, one son killed the other. Nasty stuff. Definitely not what God intended.

The Foundation Stage (Genesis 12–Judges 2:9)

God could have walked away from the human race. But he chose one man—Abraham—to begin a new nation that would belong to God alone—Israel. After Abraham, God solidified his people by setting them free from slavery, a picture of how Jesus would later rescue his people from sin. Here's where you hear God's goal for history in words that echo through the rest of the Bible: "I will take you as my own people, and I will be your God" (Exodus 6:7).

The Festering Stage (Judges 2:10–Malachi)

Uncle Fester is the guy in *The Addams Family* who looks like a wart took over his body. "Festering" is what happens if you ignore an infection in your toe until your whole leg falls off.

That's what went on through much of the rest of the Old Testament. People fled further and further from God. Sin grew worse and worse. They forgot the God who had made them and saved them, and "everyone did as he saw fit" (Judges 21:25). People once again chose not to be God's people, not because God hated them but because they hated God (Hosea 1:9).

Spot a pattern here? God made us for friendship with himself and each other. But humankind kept trashing it.

The Freedom Stage (Matthew–John)

But while humankind kept rotting in sin, God revealed a new plan. He sent a Savior—Jesus, his Son, to die the death humankind deserves. This is the part of the Bible we know well. But it's easy to forget God's goal. It's to form a new people. As Peter later told his Christian readers: "But you are a chosen people, a royal priesthood, a holy nation, a people belonging to God, that you may declare the praises of him who called you out of darkness into his wonderful light. Once you were not a people, but now you are the people of God; once you had not received mercy, but now you have received mercy" (1 Peter 2:9–10).

The Fulfillment Stage (Acts–Jude)

Early believers took the truth of what Jesus had done to their neighbors—they "evangelized" their world. Believers clustered together to form churches, then spread out to make new Christians. Sometimes God's "Good News" about Christ spread easily (Acts 2:46–47). At other times it brought persecution (Acts 5:18ff). But all the while people all over the place heard, received, and followed.

Though the Bible is written, the story isn't done. We're still living in the Fulfillment Stage. The Final Stage is yet to come.

The Final Stage (foretold in Revelation and other places in the Bible)

At the end of time as we know it, God's mammoth plan comes together. What Adam and Eve threw away at the beginning, God restores. It's paradise put back together—only better. It's heaven: "And I heard a loud voice from the throne saying, 'Now the dwelling of God is with men, and he will live with them. They will be his people, and God himself will be with them and be their God. He will wipe every tear from their eyes. There will be no more death or mourning or crying or pain, for the old order of things has passed away'" (Revelation 21:3–4). God's people spend an eternity worshipping and serving their Lord, sheltered in his care, enjoying eternal friendship with God and each other.

So here's the history of the universe in rapid review: (1) God made us for friendship with himself and with other people. (2) We broke that friendship. (3) God is working to bring us back to an eternity of friendship. (If you doubt that this is an utterly huge deal to God, look at just a few of the spots where he talks about building a people: Genesis 17:7, 12; Exodus 6:7; Leviticus 26:12; Jeremiah 31:33; Ezekiel 11:20, 36:28; 2 Corinthians 6:16; and Hebrews 8:10.)

A Message That Spreads

Building a people is the work God has been up to all along. It's *The Wave*. God wants YOU to know him. But God's plan is bigger than that. He wants OTHERS to know him too—people from all over the planet. So there's another key thing to remember about *The Wave*.

Big Swell Truth #2

God wants the people who spend eternity with him in heaven to come from every people on earth.

God's plan was never for his News about what Christ has done to hit Europe—or America—and halt. God wants worldmusic blasting through his throne room as his heavenly people shout how good he is. His people will come from every people on earth. Revelation pictures it like this: "After this I looked and there before me was a great multitude that no one could count, from every nation, tribe, people and language, standing before the throne and in front of the Lamb. They were wearing white robes and were holding palm branches in their hands. And they cried out in a loud voice: 'Salvation belongs to our God, who sits on the throne, and to the Lamb'" (Revelation 7:9–10).

That hasn't happened yet. Some people are still missing out. Some have never heard. Others have never moved on from hearing about Christ to receiving and following him. It's time for a trip to the beach to spot who those people are. That's where God is acting. It's where *The Wave* is pounding ashore.

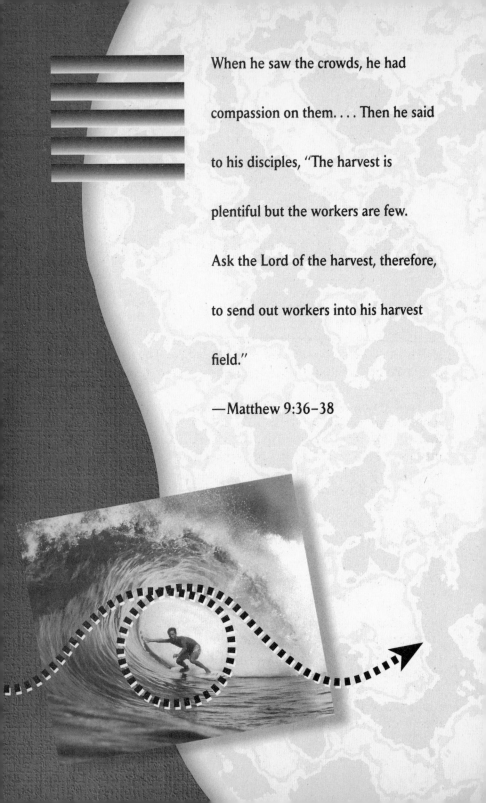

When he saw the crowds, he had compassion on them. . . . Then he said to his disciples, "The harvest is plentiful but the workers are few. Ask the Lord of the harvest, therefore, to send out workers into his harvest field."

—Matthew 9:36–38

4

Checking the Surf

It's 7:15 on a Sunday morning at Joshua's house. Josh's alarm clock explodes. His mother flings open his bedroom door. She hollers that the family leaves for church in half an hour.

Four hours ago Josh was scraping grill crud and emptying trash bins at Billy Bob's Bovine Burger Barn. At the moment, his pillow sounds way better than a pew—and the insides of his eyelids a lot more enthralling than staring at some preacher.

Josh wonders why he goes to church.

But Josh rolls out of bed like he does every Sunday morning. He knows that if he doesn't get up his parents will shovel him into the car at precisely 7:45 A.M., ready or not.

Real Christians Only

Church isn't such a bore everywhere. And in a lot of places you can't just slide into being a Christian.

Recently, for instance, eight families in India's Bihar province wanted to be baptized. But the village leader wanted one of the believers—a man named Sandhu—put to the test by standing on hot coals. While other believers prayed, Sandhu calmly stepped onto the coals and stood there for 10 minutes. (*Don't try that at home.*) Forty-seven villagers accepted Christ that day (*Advance, 3/96*).

Life as a believer doesn't always turn out so miraculously marvelous. On February 24, 1996, six believers were gunned down in a hit-and-run massacre by Muslim extremists in Azbit el-Iqbat, a village of 5,000 Christians in southern Egypt. In two weeks, 28 people died in violent attacks designed to terrorize the people and destabilize the government (*Advance, 3/96*).

There's nothing wrong with growing up in a Christian home or in a country with a church on every corner. But it can make you sloppy. Unlike the Sandhus of the world or the believers in Azbit el-Iqbat, you might not have to think about why you believe—or about some big-ticket costs of following Jesus.

And one of the worst ways you can get sloppy is to wrongly assume everyone around you is a Christian. You get a fuzzy picture of your world.

Bringing the World Into Focus

Let's get the picture into focus. How many real Christians are out there?

About *one-tenth* of the world's population of *5.6 billion people*.

One-tenth. Sound scary? From one point of view we're a puny bunch. You wouldn't want to play football all by your lonesome against nine other people—or team with nine of your friends against a mob of 90. But there's another way to look at it.

We're a lean team. That 10 percent counts only *committed* Christians—people who have aligned themselves with active, Bible-based churches. Not all of those people are all-star examples of what mature Christians can be, but they have all in some way gone beyond hearing God's Good News to receiving Jesus and beginning a life of following him.

We're a growing team. Do the numbers: It took 1,900 years for committed Christians to build to a mere 2.5 percent of the world's population. As of 1970 we had bulged to 5 percent. And by 1992 we made up 10 percent of a gigantically larger world population.

We're a big team. That 10 percent multiplied by a planetful of people is a LOT of people. Can you believe it? There're some 560 MILLION committed Christians in this world. There's a rapidly expanding crowd of people out there who are real Christians.

But there're also a whole bunch of people who aren't.

Another 20 percent of the world look like Christians but are Christians in name only—what can be called *nominal* Christians. They may claim to be Christians because they live in the sort-of Christian culture of the West. Or because their parents believed. They might practice a Christian faith mixed with other beliefs ("syncretism") or go to a brand of church that has junked biblical beliefs ("liberalism" or "universalism"). They profess to be Christians, but only God can see inside them to tell whether they have become part of his family through faith in Christ.

Chances are you know lots of nominal Christians. They might be your friends who only show up at church on Christmas Day or when someone they know is hatched, matched, or dispatched. They might go to a Christian school—but belong to the clump that would escape if they could. They're your neighbors, teachers, coaches—people all around you. To keep them straight from other people, we'll wrap nominal Christians together with committed Christians to call them *World C*.

Global ABCs

What about those who can't be called "Christian" even by the wildest stretch of the term? A whopping *70 percent* of the people in the world don't know the God of the Bible in any way. But there's an important difference between two chunks of people who make up that 70 percent:

> ☞ Some are "reached." Thirty percent of the world is non-Christians who live in cultures that have churches. They live within reach of Christians who

can tell them about Christ. Call them *World B*.

- More are "unreached." Forty percent of the world is non-Christians who live in cultures with no established church. There may be a few Christians within the culture. But they have little chance of hearing about Christ unless someone comes from outside their culture to tell them. They can be called *World A*.

Picture it this way:

10%	20%	30%	40%
Com-mitted Chris-tians	Nominal Christians	Non-Christians living in Reached Peoples	Non-Christians living in Unreached Peoples
WORLD C		WORLD B	WORLD A

Like nominal Christians, people who live in reached and unreached cultures need to hear about Christ and receive and follow him. But who's in a worse spot?

- Nominal Christians (part of World C) know the Good News but have chosen not to respond.
- People in reached cultures (World B) have neighbors nearby who can tell them about Christ.
- The nearly one billion people living in unreached cultures (World A) have a dismal chance of becoming forever friends with God. They have yet to hear how God offers them life in Christ—even once.

All three kinds of people—nominal Christians, and non-Christians in reached and unreached cultures—need to hear about Jesus. All five billion of them. Especially the ones who have never heard.

Big job. But not impossible.

Spreading the News—
The Bathrooms Are Busted

Imagine this. You're sitting at school. The principal strides to your classroom and plucks you out by name. Back in his office he explains that the school's bathrooms are broken. He has to shut school for the day. A little-known state law makes it illegal for him to keep students in school without bathrooms working. Everyone gets to go home.

Seriously. It happens.

Here's where you come in. The school's speaker system is broken. The principal gives *you* the job of telling the school. The *whole* school.

Okay. You have the urgent news. School's out. Buses are rolling in 20 minutes.

So who finds out first? People you know best. You run and tell your ten best friends. *(That's what believers have often done with God's News. They naturally go to the people they know best—people in their own or similar cultures.)*

But your job was to tell the whole school. Some of your friends have already darted for the doors, but you grab a few and send them all over the building. "Spread the news!" you tell them. *(Spreading God's News isn't a one-person job. Christians have to work together.)*

Here's where the challenges start. Some students aren't nearby. They're at the other end of the building. On athletic fields. Maybe even out on field trips. Your friends run hard to spread the news. *(God's messengers face physical boundaries—oceans, jungles, deserts, disease—though each day our world shrinks more.)*

One of your friends stumbles past the teachers' lounge. She realizes that, yes, even *they* need to know. She manages to sneak in and post messages before she's found out and booted out. *(God's messengers face political boundaries—countries that harass, stifle, or persecute Christianity. They have to find unique ways to pass on the News. More on this "creative access" later in the book.)*

Another twist. Most of your friends find people won't listen unless they spread the good news in unusual ways. People need the messengers to communicate in a way they can understand. The meeting of the mimes wants to play charades. The football players need a diagram. Home-ec students want a well-ordered list of steps to follow as they exit the building. And an English as a Second Language classroom needs your friends to talk in a dozen different languages. *(God's messengers face cultural boundaries—language, customs, and beliefs that make it less-than-easy to tell the News in an understandable way.)*

One more problem. Your friends go to each room and tell ONE person. In most rooms that works great. The mimes mime the mimes. The football players tell the football players. The home-ec students whip it up for the home-ec students. But in one room the chess club president gets the message. He's afraid to tell the jocks in the back of the class. The message halts with him. The others don't benefit from the good news. *(The job of spreading God's News isn't done until it gets to each different cultural group. And believers need to be able to tell the News for themselves to everyone around them.)*

Think People Groups

Ditch your school and zoom wide to see the world. The world's cultures fall into many blocs. We speak different languages. We live in different countries. We spring from different ethnic groups—we consider ourselves Japanese, Somali, Norwegian, Arab, Mexican, African American, Hakka Chinese, or one of thousands of other groups. When we consider all three of those tags at once—language group, national boundary, and ethnic identity—we get what Christian researchers call a "people group." All the members of a people group speak more or less the same language. They live within one country. They claim the same ethnic heritage.

The 40 percent of earthlings who live in World A aren't loners. They live in large *chunks* of people who don't know God. They live in *people groups.* (In fact, they're probably those "peoples" the Bible says will fill heaven.) Many of the world's people groups have no Christians at all. If a people group doesn't have enough Christians among them to spread God's Good News to their own people, then they're "unreached people groups" or "least-evangelized peoples." A group called Joshua Project 2000 says there are about 2.2 billion people in 1,700 least-reached groups.

So? What does math and social studies have to do with *The Wave*?

In the stupid example about broken toilets, the easiest way to spread the news is to break into large groups that can hear the message, believe it, and pass it on among themselves. *And here's the important part*: That's also the most efficient way to reach the really unreached. Telling two billion individuals would take forever. The smart first step is for Christians to start churches among each of these mostly unreached groups. It's the principle of you tell two friends and they tell two friends and they tell two friends . . . until everyone knows.

The church worldwide is pressing hard to take God's News to these culture groups. It's the driving edge of *The Wave*.

So who are these people? We could list all 1,700 least-reached peoples. (You can get an up-to-date list from Joshua Project 2000—check "Stuff in the Back of the Book" for their address.) But for now here's an easier way to figure these people out. Most of them fall into five major chunks—four religious groups, one political group. The five great unreached blocs are Tribals, Hindus, Chinese, Muslims, and Buddhists. (As Bill and Amy Stearns point out, if you flip the "C" in "Chinese" upright to make a "U," the first letters of those group names spell "THUMB.") To find out more check out chapter three of *Run With the Vision* or all of *The Compact Guide to World Religions*. (See "Stuff in the Back of the Book.")

The least-reached peoples aren't too hard to find. The group AD2000 & Beyond points out that the vast majority—90 percent—live in an area of the world they call "the 10/40 Window." It stretches from West Africa to East Asia between the 10th and 40th parallels. Check out the map!

It's startling. The 10/40 Window is where most of the events of the Old and New Testaments happened. It's home to the world's oldest civilizations. Nearly two-thirds of the world live in the 10/40 Window's 61 countries. Three of those big unreached blocs—Muslims, Hindus, and Buddhists—have strongholds there. And the poorest of the

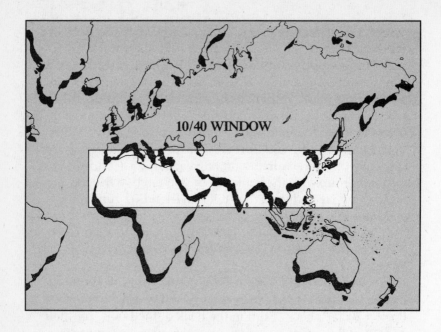

10/40 WINDOW

world's poor live there, 80 percent living on less than $500 per person a year (*AD2000 & Beyond*).

So are your non-Christian friends nearby less important than the non-Christians who live in unreached people groups? *Never. Not to God. Not to you. Never.*

But keeping track of how the church is doing in taking God's News to the least-reached peoples helps us know how we can best use our resources of prayer, money, technology, and people. And here's the crisis: Only one in ten Christian workers who go to another culture to tell God's News goes to these least-reached groups. The other nine go to cultures with strong churches (*Run With the Vision, p. 32*).

Whoever and Wherever

And that brings up one last point that's been bubbling below the surface since the first page of this book.

Jesus came to Earth and saw a world that needs to know God. "When he saw the crowds, he had compassion on them, because they were harassed and helpless, like sheep without a shepherd" (Matthew 9:36). Jesus saw a world ready to know God. "Then he said to his disciples, 'The harvest is plentiful . . .' " (9:37). Jesus saw a problem. " '. . . but the workers are few' " (9:37). *Jesus saw one solution.* "Ask the Lord of the harvest, therefore, to send out workers into his harvest field" (Matthew 9:38).

Here's the point:

Big Swell Truth #3

God uses *people* to spread the message of God's offer of life in Christ.

Non-Christians—wherever they are and whatever people group they belong to—aren't just statistics. They all have faces. Some of them are your friends.

If God has a plan to change the world and if part of his plan is to use people to accomplish his goals, then one question remains: *Are you going to be one of those people?*

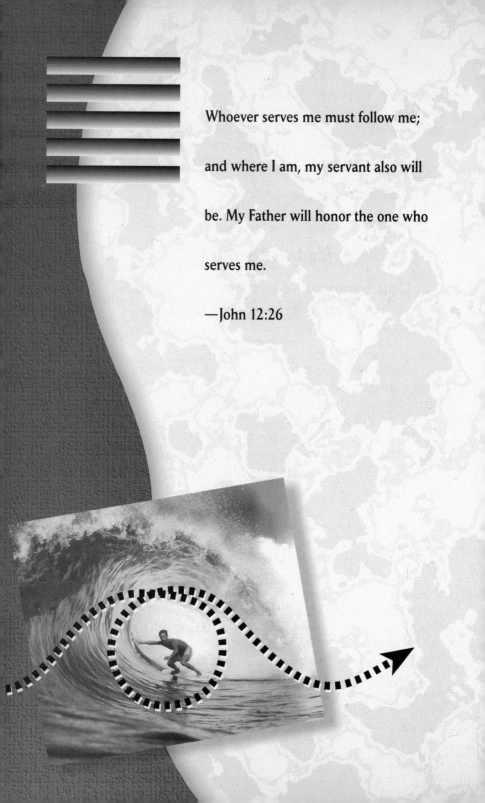

Whoever serves me must follow me;

and where I am, my servant also will

be. My Father will honor the one who

serves me.

—John 12:26

5

Born to Catch
The Wave

You stand on the shore, water licking your toes. New friends dragged you to the beach, claiming they were going to take you surfing. You try to weasel away. "It's kind of early in the year, don't you think?" They zip you into a wet suit. "I don't own a board." They loan you one. "I don't have a clue how to surf." They coach you all they can on shore.

Now it's time to get in.

Your friends surfed this spot a lot. The wind blasts across the ocean toward shore. Swells rise until they hit an undersea shelf. *Shazam.* Mammoth waves roll in.

You're stone-still as you watch water pound the shore. You have to admit it—riding the waves looks cool. Irresistable. Like you were meant to ride. But the thundering water also scares you. You worry you'll get knocked down or flipped over and slam head first or belly out on the bottom. "Just watch us," your friends reassure you.

You glance at the warm sand and the hot dog stand up the beach and ponder spending the day sunning and stuffing yourself—lots of people seem to be doing that. Why should *you* get in the water?

It's up to you. You could stay on shore. Or you could catch a wave and go for the ride of your life.

Your Place in the Plan

There are waves. And then there's THE WAVE. It's God's project to build a tight group of friends who belong to him—friends who honor him as their master and rely on his care. *The Wave* is what God is doing here, there, and everywhere. And he's using *people* to accomplish his plan.

There's no bigger wave on the face of the planet. It's the ultimate wave. And if you're a Christian, it's your destiny:

———

Big Swell Truth #4

God wants YOU to be part of his plan to reach the world.

———

God wants YOU to be a WaveCatcher. So why get in the water? Why become part of what God is doing here, there, and everywhere? Three reasons.

1. *You were born to catch The Wave.* A religious teacher once asked Jesus to name the most important thing about following God. Here's what Jesus told him: " 'Love the Lord your God with all your heart and with all your soul and with all your mind.' This is the first and greatest commandment. And the second is like it: 'Love your neighbor as yourself' " (Matthew 22:37–39). Everything else about your being a Christian flows from those two basics: Love God and love others. That's the *Great Commandment*. Allowing God to reign as King in your life means you give him and others all the love they deserve.

But God didn't intend for love to stay in one spot. He gave his people a job to do—to help other people become God's people. After Jesus rose from the grave he told his followers to "go and make disciples of all nations, baptizing them in the name of the Father and of the Son and of the Holy Spirit, and teaching them to obey everything I have commanded you" (Matthew 28:19–20). That's the *Great Commission*.

And right before Jesus left for heaven he made the *Great Prediction*. He said, "You will be my witnesses in Jerusalem, and in all Judea and Samaria, and to the ends of the earth" (Acts 1:8). His people were to *go* to tell God's News.

God never intended for his people to stand around—or to lie on the beach sunning when the real action is out in the water. Jesus spoke the Great Commandment and the Great Commission to all believers. When he made the Great Prediction he was talking about all of us. God put us together to take God's Good News of Jesus Christ to people close by and half a planet away. The whole job isn't yours. But you have a place in the plan. God gives all of us the privilege of bringing God's love to people who need to know him.

2. *God is offering you a chance to change the world.* Teachers may think you're brainless—and do nothing more than baby-sit you until graduation. Clerks may assume you're evil—and follow you around waiting for you to steal the store. Adults may say you're hopeless—and judge you by your hair, your clothes, your music, and your friends.

A lot of adults won't take you seriously. God does. A lot of adults think you're clueless. God says you're capable.

Why do you think so many of your peers toss away school, ditch their families, torch their brains with drugs? Why do they choose to destroy themselves and others? Because they've been pushed to the fringes of life. Ignored. Trivialized, neglected, and abused. They need to know that God invites them to significance. They can know him. They can do things that matter—feed a hungry person, comfort an abused child, show classmates and teachers and bosses what a real Christian looks like, help introduce people to God—and change people's lives *forever*. Life lived close to Christ is a life-altering substance, a world-changing power. God fiercely believes in them. And in you.

Working on your own you can't make a dent in the world. God working through you can change the world

49

around you. God working through you and other believers can change the planet.

Elissa spent part of her summer living at her church—clearing brush, hauling garbage, and painting houses. Here's what she says: "My friends and I were mostly 14. We did really hard work, but we didn't look at ourselves and say, 'We're too young—we can't do this.' 1 Timothy 4:12 says, 'Don't let anyone look down on you because you are young, but set an example for the believers in speech, in life, in love, in faith and in purity.' That's what we tried to do." As a young Christian you don't have to be at the bottom of the heap. You can be at the front of the pack.

3. *The time is now.* You know what it's like to work on a job that never ends—writing that term paper from you-know-where, spending half of your fifteenth year cleaning the garage, or trying to save for college on your $60-a-week part-time job. Reaching the whole world? It's just one more item on a cosmic stuff-to-do list. It seems utterly hopeless.

But it's not. Christians have drawn up some 1,100 plans to finish the task. Many are still active. None has yet succeeded. But for the first time in history it looks like we actually *can* take the Good News to all the peoples of the planet. Some feel the year 2000 or soon after is a reachable goal (visit the Web site, for example, of the AD2000 & Beyond Movement—http://www.AD2000.org).

Why is that a big deal?

Jesus said that he would return to earth only when our job is complete: "And this gospel of the kingdom will be preached in the whole world as a testimony to all nations [all peoples], and then the end will come" (Matthew 24:14). We think that Jesus promised to come again when all people groups have had the opportunity to hear God's Good News.

Dingdong. Anyone home? Get it? Finishing the job means bringing in Christ's total reign on earth, the end of the world as we know it. Much cooler than mere Sunday school. We can debate definitions of "peoples" or noodle the exact number of peoples left to reach, but the job seems more doable than ever. At some point God intends for us to achieve *closure.*

Jesus said no one can put a date or time on the end of

the world (Matthew 24:36). Jesus also said that when we see these things we will know his kingdom is near (Matthew 24:33). Maybe—just maybe—you will be part of the generation that finishes the task and ushers in Christ's return.

Plunging In

The Wave is what God is doing around the world. If that's what he's busy with, diving in is the best way to stay close to him. You can't flop on the beach or bury your head in the sand and expect to be close to him: Jesus said, "Whoever serves me must follow me; and where I am, my servant also will be" (John 12:26). Being a WaveCatcher is *good*.

You have the chance to affect the permanent destiny of people all around you. This is life or death, light or darkness, heaven or hell. And it's one sure way to get God's Angel Choir jamming: "I tell you," Jesus said, "there is rejoicing in the presence of the angels of God over one sinner who repents" (Luke 15:10). Being a WaveCatcher is *important*.

And the Beach Boys had it right: Catch a wave—and you know where you'll be sitting. Being a WaveCatcher is *cool*.

To Surf or Not to Surf

If God has a plan to change the world and if part of his plan is to use you, then one question remains: *Are you going to say yes?*

You catch *The Wave* when:

- Your heart beats with God's compassion for all the people of the world.

- You make God's purpose to reach the world your purpose.

- You decide to find your place in God's big plan.

But you have to decide to get in the water. To decide to grab your chance to change the world. To decide that *somehow* and in *some way* you will be part of God's plan.

So are you in? Think about this—and sign it if you're ready:

I Want to Catch *The Wave*!

I WANT TO OBEY
GOD'S GREAT COMMANDMENT

to love God with my whole heart and
to love other people as much as I love myself.
Matthew 22:37–39

I WANT TO FULFILL
GOD'S GREAT COMMISSION

to help all the peoples of the world hear
about Jesus and receive and follow him.
Matthew 28:18–20

I WANT TO BE PART OF
GOD'S GREAT PREDICTION

to help take the Good News about Jesus
here, there, and everywhere.
Acts 1:8

Signed _____ Date _____

So what does it mean to sign that? You're *not* signing up now to go to Ukarumpa later. You're *not* volunteering to get trampled by a rhinoceros while preaching in Africa. You're *not* even saying, "I'll go to a galaxy far, far away unless God sends a lightning bolt that forces me to stay at home."

Here's what you're saying:

I admit my whole life and my total obedience belongs to God.

I agree that spreading God's Good News is utterly important.

I promise to stick close to God and find whatever role he has for me wherever he leads.

Carpe Undam!

In the movie *Dead Poet's Society* Robin Williams plays a teacher at a prestigious prep school. One day he takes his students to a wall spread with pictures of graduates of long ago. "Move up close to the pictures," he says. "Those boys were young and intelligent and full of dreams like you. They were just like you."

Then comes the kicker. "They're all dead now," he continues. "They've turned to dust. But lean close—they're calling out to you. Listen! They're telling you, *'Carpe diem!' 'Seize the day!'* Can you hear them?"

Here's reality: Your life will pass quickly. You have to do what matters. You have to chase the one lifedream that's real and good and right. *Now* is the time to choose.

Carpe diem! Seize the day!

There's one big reason you might still stand on the shore, letting *The Wave* wash your feet, content to watch what's going on without jumping in yourself: You don't know what to do. To surf or not to surf isn't the question. You might be wondering not *if* but *how* to catch *The Wave*.

Good point. No one wants to look stupid or get tossed and eat sand. The rest of this book tells exactly *how* you can catch *The Wave*. It's time to find your place in what God is doing here, there, and everywhere.

Carpe Undam! Catch The Wave!

Offer your bodies as living

sacrifices. . . . Do not conform any

longer to the pattern of this world, but

be transformed by the renewing of

your mind. Then you will be able to

test and approve what God's will is—

his good, pleasing and perfect will.

—Romans 12:1–2

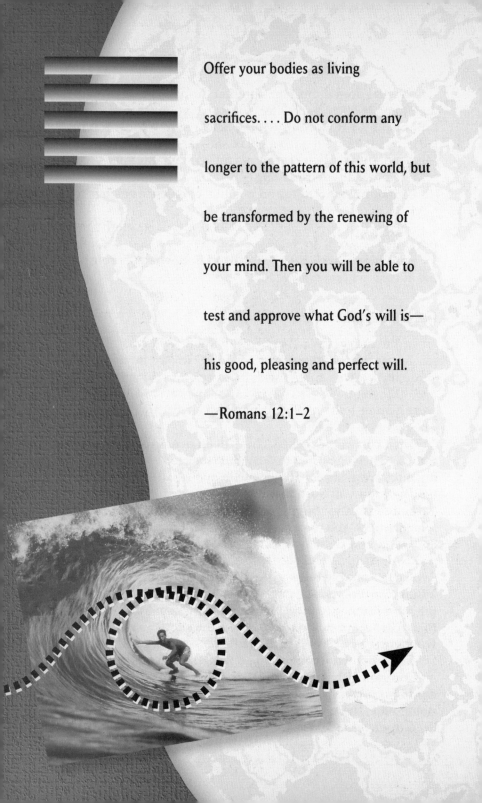

6

Grabbing Your Place in God's Plan

Erica's parents were strong Christians, but she'd never seen what a real Christian *teen* looked like. At school a pushy evangelist had cornered her once, and she knew an ugly girl who carried her Bible in front of her in angry crossed arms. Her friends at church were at best only into socializing. Nerds, crabs, fakes—no thanks. She signed up for a summer mission trip hoping there was more to God and being a Christian than that.

She boarded a bus to head off for a summer building cabins and bathrooms at a Christian youth camp in Bolivia. At the front of the bus an adult leader prayed. Outside the bus, Erica's older brother and his buddies banged on her window and made faces. They thought she was leaving to die or something. She just knew she was leaving.

Erica joined up with 33 other teens on her team—and found out that they weren't nerds, crabs, or fakes. It didn't stop there. Her teammates broke through her arrogant crust. Erica discovered that Jesus wanted and deserved her life. He wanted her to share him with others. By the end of the summer she didn't want to leave. "I don't know if I can make this work at home," she told her teammates. "I don't want to go back to the way I was. I could stay here forever."

She'd met some WaveCatchers. She'd become one.

To Infinity and Beyond

Jesus commanded his followers to tell the entire world about him (The Great Commission—Matthew 28:18–20). He pointed us to Jerusalem—our next-door neighbors. To Judea—our larger culture. To Samaria—a nearby enemy people. And to the ends of the earth—anywhere not covered by the above (The Great Prediction—Acts 1:8).

The Wave may be crashing ashore all over the world, but the world can feel a long way from where you live. The where and when and how of catching *The Wave* can overwhelm you. You worry about exactly what God wants you to do. You wonder if God can really use you:

"I can't go anywhere! I'm applying for college. The next six years of my life are planned for me."

"I went on a trip to Jamaica last summer to tell people about Christ. I want to go again—but it costs a ton of money."

"I don't have time for church stuff. My dad left us a year ago. I have to work all the time to help my mom pay the bills."

"My parents expect me to run the farm when I get older."

"Me? I'm 12. How can I reach the world? My parents won't let me go to the mall by myself."

Face it. Being a teen is like living on a leash. There's lots you can do—but a limited amount of space where you can do it. Run too far and your leash yanks tight. Run too fast and your head gets detached from your body. You'd be in a bit of trouble if you emptied your college fund and flew to

Mongolia this afternoon. You'd be guzzling yak milk and declaring God's Good News and *rude whammo*. Your mother and a Humvee full of State Department officials would pick you up by your ears and take you home.

But that's okay.

God may have incredible plans for you to serve him in exotic places. Some of those places you can get to for a summer. Others might await you in your future. Just as incredible, though, are the things you can do today or this week or ten years from now *right where you are* to be a part of God's plan. The world isn't a place you need a plane ticket to get to. It starts at your doorstep. And you don't have to be 18 or 21 (or 25 driving a rental car) to get there. You're there right now. Being a WaveCatcher is for the future *and for now*. For there *and for here*.

So what does God want from you?

Six No-Brainer Things to Do

If you're waiting for a meteor to strike and scorch a mountainside to spell out what you should do you'll wait a long time. But God made clear in the Bible most of what you need to know—what he wants you to be and do:

1. You're a Follower

When Erica returned home from Bolivia she told her best friend Keri what she had learned about following Christ totally and being a part of God's plan for the world. Keri's pastor told her that accepting Christ was enough and that following him was an extra for spiritually stoked people—not for ordinary Christians.

Dead wrong.

Following Christ up close and personal doesn't make us better in God's sight. It's the right response of a heart grateful to God and awed by his greatness. Check out what Paul wrote: "[Christ] died for all so that all who live—having received eternal life from him—might live no longer for themselves, to please themselves, but to spend their lives pleasing Christ who died and rose again for them" (2 Corinthians 5:15, TLB).

You can't be a WaveCatcher without Jesus at the center of your heart. You can get excited about travel and culture. You can cry over poverty. You can feed starving people. But you'll forget to introduce them to Jesus, the Bread of Life (John 6:35). You won't meet people's deepest needs for God.

2. You're an Example

Shelly sat staring at Mark across the lunch table. "I don't know what it is about you," she told him. "You're different from the people you hang out with. Steve and Ryan are pottymouths. You're not."

Jesus said his followers are like a city set on a hill. Its lights twinkle. It shines in the night and it's impossible to hide. Like it or don't, people will judge your God by what they see in you (Matthew 5:14–16).

Being an example is your chance to *do* something to show someone Jesus. Check out chapters 7, 8, and 9 for what you can do at church, school, and far-off places, and chapter 11 for tips on how to act so you don't make God look like a dork.

3. You're a Witness

People are watching you. And when they can see that you're different from people around you—and ask you why—they've thrown you a perfect pitch. Whack it out of the stadium. It's your chance to *say* something—to "witness."

If you saw someone run over your dog you'd shriek. It's too painful to keep quiet. God has given you new life. That's too good to hold in. Talk about it. It might be a simple "I act that way because I'm a Christian." Or it might be a bunch of long talks with someone about how he or she can become friends with God.

Non-Christians' questions, however, aren't always warmly inquisitive. They can be mean, ugly, and difficult.

Besides that, you don't have to wait for them to start the conversation. In chapter 10 we'll look at how to "give an answer to everyone who asks you to give the reason for the hope that you have . . . with gentleness and respect" (1 Peter 3:15).

4. You're a Prayer Warrior

Prayer is how you prepare the way for everything else you do. S.D. Gordon said this: "You can do more than pray after you have prayed. But you cannot do more than pray until you have prayed. Prayer is striking the winning blow at the concealed enemy; service is gathering up the results of that blow among the men and women we see and touch." Chapter 11 tells how and why to pray for your world.

5. You're a Sender

Unless you're unbelievably wealthy you probably can't foot the bill to send full-time workers to Vanuatu (that's near Australia). But check your church's bulletin boards for picture postcards of missionaries your church already supports financially. Those people need prayer, fan mail, and an occasional jar of Cheez Whiz. Write often, pray more, and find out how to send a care package.

What you lack in money you make up for in brains and energy. One great possibility for your long-distance care is being a pen-pal or e-mail pal to missionary kids your own age.

If you don't find those postcards then ask your pastor whether your church supports any missionaries. (If he or she laughs at you and asks what a missionary is, find another church. No foolin'. Look for a church that cares about God's cause worldwide. You might want to contact a group called ACMC and see if they have any member churches in your area. Their address is in "Stuff in the Back of the Book.")

More on sending in chapter 12.

6. You might be a Goer

God gives some people the job of *going*. As in leaving home. Not for college or something—but to take God's News to another culture. In chapters 9 and 12 you'll find out more about how you can take the message to another part of the world as a short-term or a long-term messenger.

Still Waiting?

You don't have to wait for God to tell you. When you belong to him you're a *Follower* . . . an *Example* . . . a *Witness* . . . a *Prayer Warrior* . . . a *Sender* . . . and maybe a *Goer*. God knows what you can do and when you can do it. He sees your own personal present and future. Here are some things you can count on for your whole life:

What God wants you to accomplish WON'T change. Your task is the same no matter where you are or how old you are. You're to help build God's people. It's your job to help others (1) hear about Christ, (2) receive his forgiveness, and (3) follow him.

The role you play in God's plan WILL change. How you fit in his plan changes every time you change. With every skill or fact you learn, every spiritual lesson you master, every way you mature, your capacity to be used by God grows. The Bible warns that you shouldn't pretend to fully know your future (James 4:13–17). That goes for the role you play in God's work. You can only draw a road map of your life after you've walked it. Again—that's okay. God wants you to develop trust in him by following him. Each good choice is another step forward in his plan.

Where you work toward God's goals WILL change. School, jobs, apartments, a house and a spouse, children, sickness, health—they all impact how and where God can use you. That's life.

———

What God wants from you is this: to serve him at all times and in all places to your fullest. Being a WaveCatcher means you make yourself totally available to God wherever you are. Paul explained it like this:

> Therefore, I urge you, brothers, in view of God's mercy, to offer your bodies as living sacrifices, holy and pleasing to God—this is your spiritual act of worship. Do not conform any longer to the pattern of this world, but be transformed by the renewing of your mind. Then you will be able to test and approve what God's will is— his good, pleasing and perfect will.
>
> Romans 12:1–2

You could put on a Christian T-shirt and run in front of a bus and make yourself a traveling human billboard for Christ. But God don't want no dead sacrifices. He would rather have you *live* for him wherever you go. God reveals his plans for you as you go along—as you

accept his mercy and care for you
offer yourself to him
live up to what you know, and
think about the world the way he thinks.

That's how you find out exactly what God wants of you. That's how you find and keep finding your place in his plan.

Therefore, as we have opportunity,

let us do good to all people,

especially to those who belong to the

family of believers.

—Galatians 6:10

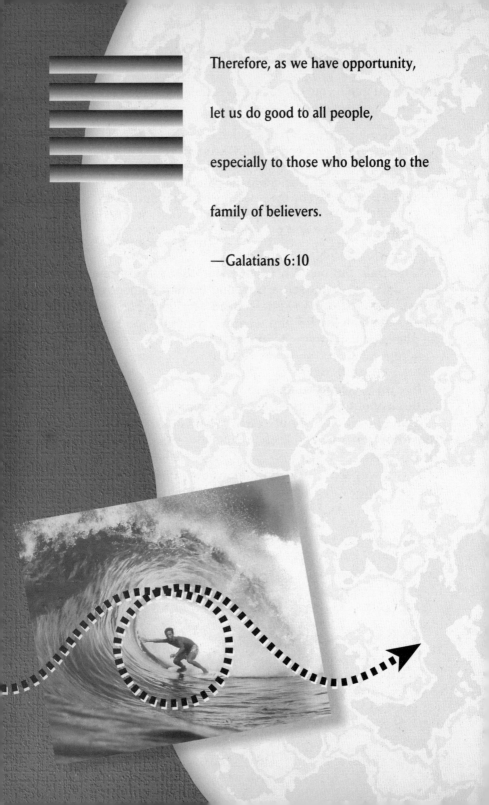

7

Lead, Follow, or Get in the Way

Picture this. You're bored. But you live close to Chicago. Oodles to do. So you: (a) hit the local amusement park, the one guaranteed to shock your brain into sensory overload; (b) cruise the lakefront, with its miles of cycling and skating paths; (c) take in Chicago's primo museum of art—or natural history, or science—or the aquarium with an octopus so cute you want to let it suction itself permanently to your brain; (d) enjoy the local fine dining—let some White Castle hamburgers slide down your esophagus, eat one of those lard-o-rific Chicago hot dogs, or inhale spinach pizza at Gino's East—don't forget markers to write on the wall; (e) go see the Cubbies, Bears, or Bulls; or (f) start a Sunday school.

If you're a normal human being between the ages of 4 and 92, option (f) is probably last on your bust-the-boredom list.

Maybe it shouldn't be.

As a youth pastor in Wheaton, Illinois, Ridge Burns scouted out a tough 1,200-resident apartment complex in nearby Carol Stream. Of the complex's 200 children under age ten, 120 were latchkey kids. When Ridge saw a group of those young kids step off a school bus to face one more afternoon on their own, he cried.

A 16-year-old in Ridge's group had been aching to "do something big for God." The vision Sue Bolhouse caught was caring for these kids after school. One problem: The only realistic way to work with the kids was to cough up hundreds of dollars of monthly rent for an apartment. So the students in Ridge's high school group pledged their own money and rented an apartment to house a program. Not much later Sue was leading 60 of her peers in a five-day-a-week combo Big Brother-Big Sister/Vacation Bible School/Tutoring program. Students met the kids at the school buses and took them to the apartment for singing, games, crafts, and Bible stories. They called it "Sidewalk Sunday School." (You can find out more about what these students accomplished in a book by Ridge Burns and Pam Campbell called *Create in Me a Youth Ministry, pp. 139–158*. See "Stuff in the Back of the Book.")

Sue and her friends did *what* they could *where* they could—more than anyone *thought* they could. And they didn't wait until they turned 21.

A Garage Kinda Band

So you want to reach the world. Where do you start?

When you and your friends form a band you don't start by playing stadiums and burning CDs by the bazillion. You practice. In the garage. With the door down—PUH-LEEAZE! You *could* practice with the door up. You'd blow eardrums. You'd look cool for the neighborhood. But you'd spend your energy on stage moves rather than music. And the neighbors would call the cops. Better to close the door, make some noise, and get things done.

The church is your garage. It's a place to build courage, love, and conviction. Three points:

1. *Church is where you train.* If you can't make your faith work there—if you can't put what you believe into practice through caring about your Christian family—you won't do well trying to show Christ to the world. John wrote, "If anyone says, 'I love God,' yet hates his brother, he is a liar. For

anyone who does not love his brother, whom he has seen, cannot love God, whom he has not seen" (1 John 4:20). In the same way, if you claim to love people far away but don't love those nearby—brothers and sisters in God's family you see at least once a week—you're a liar. God wants us to "do good to all people, especially to those who belong to the family of believers" (Galatians 6:10).

2. *Church is where you're stuck together to other believers.* You can't be a band by yourself. And God gave each of us Christians different gifts that we need to work together. (Check out Romans 12:6–8; 1 Corinthians 12–14; Ephesians 4:12–16 for some lists of gifts and how they work together.) Depending on other Christians is the only way you'll fully mature or change the world.

3. *Church is where you plot how to carry out God's plan.* Psalm 67 says this: "May God be gracious to us and bless us and make his face shine upon us, that your ways may be known on earth, your salvation among all nations. . . . God will bless us, and all the ends of the earth will fear him" (Psalm 67:1–2, 7).

God has given us much. Forgiveness. Love. Protection. Membership in his family. He didn't mean for us to hog him. He gives to us so we can give to others—he "blesses us so we can be a blessing." God builds up the church. The church reaches out *here* to its own people. It stretches to help over *there*—to non-Christians nearby. And it goes *everywhere* Christians haven't gone before—to non-Christians living at the ends of the earth. It takes all of us working together.

Lead, Follow, or Get in the Way

Nothing's wrong with having the usual kind of wacky youth group fun. Unless it's all you do—or even the major part of your activities. You can be more than a bunch of roller-coaster animals. And you sure don't have to settle for destroying the youth room and the rest of the church. Punchin' and smokin' and rippin'. Holes in walls and pot in stairwells and doors off bathroom stalls. Like Sue Bolhouse and the students who took Sunday school to an apartment complex, you can accomplish way more than most people think.

The rest of this chapter lists things you can do to start right where you are to get in the water and catch *The Wave*. Some are up-front jobs—others are behind-the-scenes. Some you do with a lot of people—others you can work more on your own. Some are in the church—others push past the walls to reach out to non-Christians.

Training the Troops

The church doesn't do anyone any good if it doesn't make disciples—people who know, honor, and follow Christ. Here are some ways you can help:

Teach Sunday School. Everybody has a Sunday school. Almost everybody is shorthanded. Besides—you probably have a zillion ideas to make Sunday school hum. (Just keep them to yourself for a while.) Offer to help with crowd control, stories, crafts, music, games, sports, skits, moving kids around, taking attendance and offerings. You can lead or just be an enthusiastic participant. If no one will take you as a volunteer, then talk your parents into teaching and help them. Teaching works best if you're at least two or three years older than the kids you teach. Don't be more work to the teacher than you're worth.

Like the adults, you'll need to figure out a way to juggle teaching and worship and your own Sunday school. Watch the adults and find out what they do.

Baby-sit. Work in the nursery during worship services and special events. Get Red Cross certified. (Baby-sitting is an ideal place to start—everyone knows you can care for kids. But don't let them lock you in the nursery if there are other jobs you want to try around the church.)

Be a Youth Leader. Think of it. You—the model of godliness. Help with students younger than you, whether that's junior highers or elementary kids. You can be a mentor, lead a small group, or assist in mid-week Bible studies or programs like Awana, Christian Service Brigade, or Pioneer Clubs.

Help at a Vacation Bible School. Or grab some help and start one. Lots of VBSs are dying because adults won't do them. Contemplate this: It's your tan or a kid's soul.

Lead Worship. Do more than light the candles. Don't settle for a once-a-year Youth Sunday (the adults know when you're coming and turn down their hearing aids). Be a part of services as often as you can. Do music or drama, read Scripture, help with the sound or lighting systems. In some churches you can help serve communion—a pretty awestriking thing. You can pitch in and liven up your own Bible studies and Sunday school classes.

Assist With Special Needs Kids and Adults. If your church has a Special Ed class for adults, volunteer to help. Or help one-on-one with kids in the Sunday school program who need extra attention. You'll keep the regular teachers sane and care for special kids the way Christ does.

Stocking the Supply Line

The church won't work if people don't pitch in to meet practical needs. Lots of these tasks you can do in different places—you might do them for kids, for your youth group, or for the wider church.

Get People to Church. Plenty of parents won't take the time to get their kids to one more thing. Drive—probably a good idea to have your license—or get your parents to drive. Use the time in the car to talk real with your friends.

Cook. Where two or three Christians are gathered a snack will be served. Make it happen.

Greet. Make it your job to welcome kids to Bible study or Sunday school, or join the adults who say hi and hold the doors for worshipers on Sunday morning.

Publish a Newspaper or Newsletter. Start a newspaper by youth for youth. Write. Photographize. Interview. Get the inside scoop. You'll take a burden off your adult youth leaders and get your group organized.

Work on Church Mailings. Help in the office. Stuff Envelopes. Fold Bulletins. Photocopy. Any job you do means church secretaries are free for other work.

Compute. You have more computer knowledge in your trigger thumbs than most adults have in their whole body. You can set up databases and even spreadsheets. You can desktop publish or set up a Web page or news group for the youth or the church as a whole.

Get on a Committee. Join the missions committee and find out how you can help or pray. Look into other committees. Just make sure you're actually interested in what the committee does—do you really care what color they paint the basement bathrooms? And make sure the adults aren't patting you on the head by letting you join.

Wash Toys in the Nursery. Think gumming babies and toddler spit and scrub away.

Clean. Volunteer to vacuum. Do windows on Saturday so people have something to fingerprint on Sunday. Then the church can spend money on something other than a cleaning crew—like sending workers to unreached peoples. You can get in on doing room setups, grounds keeping (don't say you don't know how to run a lawn mower), and painting. If the adults won't do these jobs show them up. It's good for them.

Clean Up. Don't leave it to your youth pastor to pick up candy wrappers and soda cans after you meet. He's getting old and he can't bend down so good anymore.

Make a Media Splash. In a smaller church "media ministry" means you know how to get the words right-side-up on the overhead. A bigger church might be running TV cameras, video toasters, and complicated platform lighting. (You may run tech crew for school dramas—who says you can't do it at church?) In any size youth group you can shoot photos, assemble slide shows, or edit videos.

Plan Outings. If you can call a theater to find out when a movie is showing and manage to get four friends to the same spot at the same time, you can set up events for your group or church. Call places, get prices, make handouts and posters.

Team Up With Your Pastor. Find out what it's like to meet people's daily hurts. Ask to go on some hospital calls. Both he and the people you visit will freak.

Ush. It's a lot like asking your parents for money.

Count the Offering. You may count out a till at work containing mucho money. People do need their privacy in what they give—but you can at least count the cash and sort coins. It's a tad sad that your pagan employer trusts you with thousands of dollars but your church won't. Bring that up. Then duck.

Advancing the Front Lines

A church dies if it never moves beyond its walls. The Sidewalk Sunday School was spectacular because students didn't wait for the kids to come to them. They went to where the kids were at. Here are some ways to break down the walls without leaving your city.

You can be a part of what Christians are probably already doing all around you:

Community Evangelism. Do drama and music anywhere and everywhere, or do other forms of evangelism your church does—street witnessing, door-to-door, visiting visitors.

Urban Ministries. Get involved in youth centers, Bible studies, church starts, teaching people to read.

Youth Outreaches. You name it—use sports, tutoring, Vacation Bible Schools, Big Brother and Big Sister programs, Sidewalk Sunday School, concerts.

Runaway Shelters. Ask your pastor who's doing what.

Prolife Ministries. Ditto.

Community Outreaches. Be creative—like car clinics for single moms.

Hunger Awareness. Help at homeless shelters, food pantries, clothes closets, or in building homes for the poor.

Pregnancy hotlines. Woman the phones.

Refugee Sponsorship. Find things we take for granted, like refrigerators, beds, and couches. Teach English.

Adopt-a-Highway Cleanups. Wear blaze orange. Refrain from trying to resuscitate dead animals.

And some more ideas:

Get on the Air. Use amateur radio to help missionaries—

your church probably has a ham operator who could help. Get a Christian rock segment on a local station or start a low-power neighborhood station at your church. Start small. But think high wattage.

Visit Shut-Ins. Don't go to sing songs at Christmas—if you're not going to show up the rest of the year, that is. Ditto for nursing homes. You can bring pets, music, skits, and games. Clean. Do chores and other shopping. And chat. You're better than a ChiaPet.

Throw a Birthday Party for Jesus at Christmas. Have church kids invite friends.

Collect Mittens. And jackets, clothes, shoes, care packages, and Christmas presents. Do it for inner-city kids, children of prison inmates, or people on the other side of the planet. One church sent enough clothing to start a store in Romania that funded several pastors.

Sponsor a Kid. Compassion International, World Vision, and many other groups enable you to provide a child with clothing, food, clean water, and an education. If you can't swing the monthly pledge, chip in with your family or friends. (See "Stuff in the Back of the Book.")

Starve for a While. World Vision provides materials to do a *30-Hour Famine*, a fundraiser for hunger. (See "Stuff in the Back of the Book.")

Getting the Job Done

See? You don't have to leave home to change your world.

Church is your chance to *follow*. To do what others already do. That's the way it's supposed to be. You shouldn't have to start from scratch.

But sometimes church is your chance to *lead*. To do what others won't—like jobs adults think are beneath them. Press on. Be respectful about it, but do what's right and drive them crazy with guilt!

And at times church will be your chance to *get in the way*. To do what others can't. You can put your unique gifts and enthusiasm into action, like the students who made Sidewalk Sunday School fly.

Got some ideas now? Maybe you found yourself in the lists above and saw something to do right here, right now.

But maybe not. You didn't like anything in these lists. Outstanding! Start something new. Get in our way. Get our attention. Show us where *The Wave* is breaking. But don't stand on the shore and moan that there's nothing to do.

Dear friends, I urge you, as aliens and strangers in the world, to abstain from sinful desires. . . . Live such good lives among the pagans that, though they accuse you of doing wrong, they may see your good deeds and glorify God on the day he visits us.

—1 Peter 2:11–12

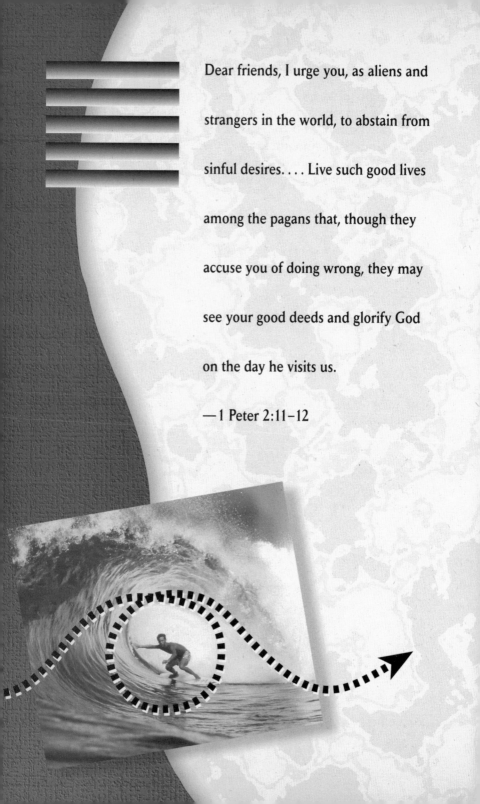

8

Be True to Your School

It was a staggering honor. Toward the end of a long school day your first-grade teacher picked you to clap the blackboard erasers. But there was more. Mrs. Heffermeister chose you not only to clap the erasers but to whap them. As the exalted Guardian-of-the-Erasers you strutted to the custodians' shop to use the whap-o-matic machine. Deftly you sucked the chalk from the erasers with a *whapity whapity whapity whoooosh.*

You returned to your classroom triumphant, an armful of clean erasers held before you. You knew you'd won Mrs. Heffermeister's heart. Oh, to see that wide grin dimple her plump face once again.

But you'd whapped one too many erasers. Your classmates glared. The next day at recess they taunted you: "Teacher's Pet—Teacher's Pet." You weren't sure what it meant. Except that it had to do with being dumb, drooly, and too eager to please.

Whether you grew up clapping erasers or wiping down

whiteboards, at some point it stopped being cool to be good at school.

You don't go to school because of a plot between your principal, parents, and teachers. Really. You're there because it's God's place for you—the spot in the here, there, and everywhere he sends you five days a week. God's plan to reach the world includes your school. But you don't like getting laughed at. Or beat up. Ignored. Being uninvited to parties. So maybe you choose to duck between your conscience and your classmates. Maybe you aim to be good enough to calm your conscience but not so good you get noticed.

That's settling for playing in the shadows when you could be living in the light. It's living a lie when you belong to the truth. Remember 1 Peter 2:9–10—where Peter says that you're part of God's people, that you belong to God, and that you've been called out of darkness into light? Right after those words Peter points out how your belonging to God affects how you live:

> Dear friends, I urge you, as aliens and strangers in the world, to abstain from sinful desires, which war against your soul. Live such good lives among the pagans that, though they accuse you of doing wrong, they may see your good deeds and glorify God on the day he visits us.
>
> 1 Peter 2:11–12

You don't always fit with your world because your real home is heaven—why would a living soul feel at home in a graveyard? When you follow what's right—God's way—the good life you live gets noticed. Even people who say you do wrong will someday admit that you're right. And that your God is Ultimate Power, Ultimate Intelligence, Ultimate Justice, and Ultimate Love.

It's time to show your school who Jesus is. Public school, home school, Christian school—you can live in a way that people "see your good deeds and glorify God."

Make It Cool to Be Good at School

You could suddenly blurt what you believe at the people at school. It's better to show *and* tell. Your classmates want more than words and your actions make your words believable. Check out a bunch of ways you make it cool to be good at school:

Hang Together

You might know only a handful of Christians at your school. (If you don't know any, start praying for some.) You may not be tight friends. But you have the chance to *daily* push each other forward in your faith. Whether or not you go to the same church, make it your goal to hang together. Your classmates will know you follow Christ by the way you care for each other with Christ's unselfish love (John 13:34–35).

Meet together. Going to church is great. But the church isn't a building—it's people. You're the church when you're walking the halls. By meeting before or after school or at lunch with other Christians you have a powerful chance to be built together, make a statement on campus, and pray for your friends. You can search the Bible together to find out what's right and then encourage each other to stand strong.

Pray at the pole. Each fall the National Network of Youth Ministries puts on "See You At The Pole" to pull Christian students together at their schools' flagpoles to pray for students, teachers, and administrators. It's no small deal. In 1995, 2.5 *million* students around the world took part. The event gives you a chance to spot other believers, form friendships, and plot how to reach your school. NNYM can also tell you if there's a youth worker in your area able to help you spread God's News at your school. (See "Stuff at the Back of the Book.")

Do a before-school program. Most Christian groups at school are Bible studies or prayer groups aimed at Christians. But some groups fill the gym one morning a week with a program for non-Christians featuring hot music and smarter-than-your-average talks.

Spread Out

"God called us to live and reach out to others," Donn—a college freshman—says about what he learned about showing Christ to his high school. "I've learned that those kids that are most difficult are the ones Christ came for. He didn't come for people who think they're healthy and 'good,' but for the ones that everyone else sees as worthless."

Christians sometimes act like an igloo—toasty on the inside and frosty on the outside. Or a clique—a circle turned inward. Jesus made the same point Donn does. When religious people accused Jesus of being too tight with sinners, he replied, "It is not the healthy who need a doctor, but the sick. . . . For I have not come to call the righteous, but sinners" (Matthew 9:12–13). Half of your job is to stick together with other Christians. The other half is to spread out. It's the only way you can keep God's News from getting stuck with you.

Tear down the walls. Your school has cultural barriers as big as any that full-time missionaries find. More often than not the problem isn't the size of the walls but the size of your fears. Everyone from the nerds to the cheerleaders named Buffy and Muffy needs to know about God. Go over the top. Fear no one but God (Luke 12:4–5).

Keep up your friendships. One of the easiest ways to break down walls is to demolish the ones you helped build. Stay friends with old friends—like the kid who's devolved into a drug-crazed caveman. Start by saying hi again.

Break the color code. God loves all peoples. There are pieces of every culture that anger him. Reject stereotypes and step outside your own world. How many of your friends are of a different race than you?

Be a welcomer. The Bible hits hard on the importance of kindly treating "aliens," newcomers from other cultures (Exodus 23:9). "Welcomers" are WaveCatchers who focus not on *going* to another culture but on *welcoming* people who come to their own. Learn about the other cultures in your school. Instead of making fun of exchange students and immigrants and kids of migrant workers, make friends with them.

Host an exchange student. Looking for something more? Get your parents to take a student from another country short-term or for a school year. Check with the school office or your church.

Bring them to your world. Shock your non-Christian friends by bringing them into a world where people don't rip each other to pieces. Build a caring youth group at church where you can be proud to invite people.

Stand Out

You have a thousand chances a day to be different from your classmates—not to be weird, but to live the way Christ wants, loving him and others. Sometimes you'll stand alone. When you stick with what's right you'll often start a crowd.

Care about people and listen to them. Thor graduated from high school last year with Donn. "I impacted my school by walking my talk," he says. "I tried to show how Christians are people who care about others and aren't just preaching that everyone is going to hell. People must have noticed because they voted me prom king and 'best personality' in the yearbook."

Clean the hamster cage. You probably don't have a cage of hamsters in the back of your classroom. But remember the principle: Do the dirty work. Clean up after yourself in shop. Bus your tray at lunch. Resist the temptation to thonk a piece of clay on your art teacher's forehead. Little things matter.

Show up for class. Some teachers don't seem to know when they're filling the room with hot air and putting everyone to sleep. They're oblivious to which students have cut class and propped up paper-mache dummies in their place. But most teachers know if you're there and you're listening. If you don't have the courtesy to listen to them, they'll never listen to you.

Make your body a drug-free zone. Don't Be A Dork Rule #1: Everyone in your school can name the people who party on Saturday and go to church on Sunday.

Show them what True Love looks like. Don't Be A Dork Rule #2: Everyone in your school can name the people who sleep around on Saturday and go to church on Sunday.

Forgive. Forgive like God forgives you (Colossians 3:13). The Bible says that when you leave revenge to God you heap burning coals on your enemy's head (Romans 12:20). Sounds better than whatever you thunk up.

Be kind. If you don't have anything nice to say . . . (Ephesians 4:29).

Keep it clean. Where would your toothbrush rather be—in a toilet or in your mouth? (Ephesians 5:3).

Play fair. Don't break legs. Don't cuss at the coach. Don't headbang the referee.

Keep your promises. God doesn't lie. Why should you? (Titus 1:2).

Throw great parties. If you don't know how to have clean fun, then you and your Christian friends really are as boring as everyone says. Find out what kind of fun you can have *inside* God's boundaries.

Share your parents. You may think your parents are strange. Chances are that if you're a decent human being, your parents are too. The biggest gift you might ever give your friends is to let them get to know adults who care about you—and them.

Speak Up

James says we should be "quick to listen, slow to speak and slow to become angry" (James 1:19). That goes for school. When you disagree, make sure you know what you disagree with. Your non-Christian teachers and any students with brains won't respect what *you* say if you don't understand what *they* say about big issues like evolution, relativism, and multiculturalism.

Speak up in class. It's your job to master material—and it isn't selling out to parrot it back. You can, however, *add* what you think at the end of your answer, whether in class or on a test. Check out the books listed in chapter 10 for ways to answer objections to Christianity wisely.

Don't feel alone. A *lot* of Christians teach in public schools. They care about students. But they aren't free in most schools to openly share their beliefs. If you pay attention, though, you'll discover who they are. They're wise friends.

Write for the school paper. Find out what free speech really means. What does it mean when you want to say something? What does it mean when your opponents say something you know is wrong or spiritually stupid?

Think long term. You aren't the first Christian to pass through your public school. Anything you can *say* your teachers have heard before. But there's something they may not have *seen*: a Christian who lives his or her faith to graduation and beyond. You may have to wait fifteen years to have a talk that makes a difference in a teacher's life.

Fair is fair. Your non-Christian teachers or principals or school board members are *not* the enemy. We have *one* enemy (Ephesians 6:12). Listen for points where you agree. And never forget that the people who got Jesus the maddest weren't "sinners" but religious hypocrites. So who are most of your non-Christian teachers steamed at? Religious hypocrites. Don't be one. If the Christian shirt doesn't fit, don't wear it.

Make a Splash

Paul wrote to the Corinthians to help them sort out gray areas—points where real believers disagreed about what was right to do. He said that in many areas of life believers are free to do as they please. He warned them to do nothing that made weak believers stumble. And then he told them to burn one principle into their brain: "So whether you eat or drink or whatever you do, do it all for the glory of God" (1 Corinthians 10:31). You can't find a rule or a recommendation in the Bible for everything. But you do "all for the glory of God" when you act in a way that shows his greatness and love:

Beat them at their own game. For all those people who think Christians are stupid, make it a goal to prove them wrong. Make it a goal to graduate at the top of your class.

If you can't be the best, then do your best. Do your best at whatever you do. Lead well. Follow well. Study hard.

Plan alternatives. Find what's good and throw yourself

into it. Or propose an alternative—like planning alcohol-free activities after prom. Don't whine about evil. Replace it with good.

Volunteer. It's sad if you let non-Christians outdo you in doing good. Pitch in at school and beyond: Tutor young kids. Be a peer counselor or mediator. Work with the homeless. Recycle. Collect for food drives. Run, bike, or bowl for charity. Donate blood. Register voters. Don't let the fact that you can't do everything be an excuse for doing nothing.

Be True to Your School

Your school is your place to spread God's News five days a week. And your school—even most Christian schools—is a building on fire with pain. *Choice 1*: You stand by and let your school burn to the ground. *Choice 2*: You hide by a drinking fountain and squirt water and maybe save a few square feet close by. Or *Choice 3*: You grab a hose and battle to save your school.

You can choose to not care. You can choose to be so quiet no one knows you're there. But if you want to turn a turbohose on the flames, then you need to choose to live what you say you believe. Listen to Donn: "Thor and I started the Bible study, lived and stood for what we believed. . . . By letting people know where we stood they knew something was different and would talk to us about things that they might not with others. . . . By living what we believed, people saw something different. They commented a lot that they wished they could have that too."

People notice when you don't live for God.

They also notice when you do.

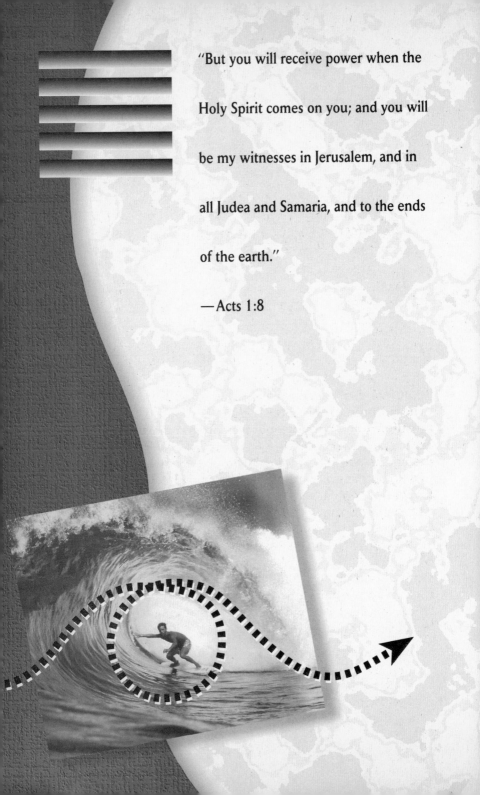

"But you will receive power when the Holy Spirit comes on you; and you will be my witnesses in Jerusalem, and in all Judea and Samaria, and to the ends of the earth."

—Acts 1:8

9

Pushing the Edge

When Daniel Hahn led a group of high school students who sang, acted, and mimed across Europe telling people about Christ, they went to places you don't see on postcards.

"One evening in Berne, Switzerland, I visited an outdoor Red Cross clinic set on the edge of a park," Daniel writes. "The purpose of this mobile clinic is to aid drug addicts, prostitutes, and street people. The program includes giving addicts low dosages of heroin in clean needles in an effort to stem the tide of AIDS and crime as well as the prostitution that accompanies addiction. As I sat there with this beaten crowd of people it struck me afresh why Jesus came. I sat with one woman who was actually shooting up as a I spoke with her" (*Mission Hills Church—Europa 1995*).

When people push God out of their lives, they create a world of hurt. It's a world that needs to hear about Christ, receive his forgiveness, and follow his fresh way of life. *They* need to hear. And *you* don't have to wait to be an adult to tell them. Check out a few of the places teenagers went one recent summer to explain God's News:

Albania • Appalachia • Australia • Bahamas • Belize • California • Canada • Chicago • Costa Rica • Czech Republic • Ecuador • Fiji • Florida • Germany • Guatemala • Houston • Italy • Jamaica • Jordan • Kenya • Los Angeles • Madagascar • Malawi •

Mexico • Micronesia • Mozambique • Nepal •
Pakistan • Papau New Guinea • Philippines •
Portugal • Siberia • Thailand • Venezuela • Vietnam •
Washington, D.C. • Zimbabwe.

Too many places to list! And the variety of *what* groups do is just as long—all with the purpose of telling God's love in word and action:

Baby-sitting • Balloons • Biking • Building churches •
Church services • Cleaning • Constructing schools •
Cooking • Counseling • Crafts • Dance • Digging •
Distributing tracts • Drama • Encouraging local
believers • Evangelistic Bible studies • Feeding the
hungry • Friendship evangelism • Handing out
Bibles • Health clinics • Hiking • Mime • Music •
Orphanage work • Painting • Prison outreaches •
Puppets • Rehabbing houses • Sports ministries •
Starting churches • Teaching English • Testimonies •
Vacation Bible Schools.

It used to be that anyone who went anywhere to spread God's News went for life. Now you can go anytime you're paroled from school—weekends, spring break, Christmas or summer vacations. Someone somewhere will get you there—and back.

Just Say Go

God has put you in your own Jerusalem (Acts 1:8). It's where you live from day to day. But you can also be a part of going to Samaria and the ends of the Earth *now*

If you've told God that you want to catch *The Wave*, you probably dream about chances to go with God to the ends of the planet—you *just say go.* Not everyone thinks that way. Some Christians hear "short-term missions" and shudder— they *just say no.* They have a long list of objections why teens and other "short-termers" have no place in God's plan to reach the world—at least not the far-off peoples of the world.

You might be eager to go. You may have already gone. You might even be on a trip as you read this book. In any case, you need to hear their worries—and work hard to prove them wrong. Here's what they think:

1. *You aren't a real messenger.* It's true that if you go as a teenager you're not mature to the max, trained to the hilt, and signed up for life. You may not be fully aware of the serious sacrifices made by God's messengers of the past—like the many who stood on the decks of ships and waved as they sailed off, knowing they were leaving home to face certain death in the Americas or Africa or Asia.

But God has given all of us the task of spreading his News. If you're friends with God then he has given you the job of introducing him to others—especially those who know little about him. Even the freshest of believers can be his "ambassadors, as though God were making his appeal through us" (2 Corinthians 5:17–20).

It's true that some short-termers are bratty tourists. Some are global power-shoppers. Some turn into short-term junkies who crave trip after trip and never find a long-term place in God's plan. But you can take the real message. You can do real ministry. Just because you're young doesn't mean you have to be a real jerk.

2. *You don't understand the culture.* Waving the wrong way in another culture might mean you want to make trouble—or make out. Accepting the wrong dinner invitation may mean you just said "yes" to getting engaged. Culture can be a puzzle. But any smart long-term worker you work with can tell you sixteen things not to do or say in a particular setting.

This protest is losing its punch in our shrinking world. You're growing up in a global youth culture. Kazakstan gets better cable stations than you do. Even suburban America isn't monochromatic—one color—a place where everyone looks and acts and believes the same. You're forced to practice "cultural sensitivity" every time you go to school.

3. *You cost too much money.* Going for a few weeks to a far-off place does cost thousands of dollars. What it costs you

to go for a summer might support several local workers for a year. Yow!

You do have to question the sense of projects that fly you to Mount Everest for a week or a weekend. Most of the cost is airfare. The longer you stay the more you accomplish for the money. And people rightly expect you to work—not goof off.

But chew on this. Suppose the adults in your church spend $3,000 to send you somewhere this summer. *Possibility 1*: You go back there or to another place to serve long-term. God's cause gains a long-term worker. *Possibility 2*: You don't return. But the short-term trip will probably make you a WaveCatcher for life, and the money spent on you is paid back many times through the money, time, and energy you pour back into God's cause over your lifetime.

You're an investment!

4. *You'll be in danger you won't be able to handle.* Many short-term trips take you out of your comfort zone. You go to strange places. You see drug dealers, hunger, disease, drunkenness, spiritual darkness. It can be physically and emotionally rough.

Welcome to the world. Your grandparents or parents maybe risked everything to move to another country for freedom and opportunity—and they did it at your age or younger. There's no need to be stupid. There are places where missionaries even now risk being kidnapped and killed. But you don't have to be unnecessarily scared. See "Better to Know *Before* You Go" in this chapter for answers to your parents' and others' legitimate concerns.

5. *You get in the way of real missionaries.* You do if you show up on their doorstep unprepared and uncoached. But go with someone who has gone before. Do what they tell you. Not only will you *not* get in the way, you can do things the long-term folks can't do. You can teach a Vacation Bible School, put together a team of basketball players that can attract some real attention, or sing or do major street dramas. You can bring energy and visibility they need.

Why You *Should* Go

Why you *shouldn't* go is far from the whole story. Maybe you've already gone. Or you've heard how great it is. Listen to all the reasons why you *should* go from some teenagers who've been there:

To learn to boldly share what you believe: "I've learned how to reach out and talk to people and trust that God will speak through me. . . . I've learned to be bold with my faith even when it seems out of the norm." (Michelle)

To meet people different from you: "A homeless man who was drunk was lying in the street listening, and a lady who lived with him got him up and got him over to the side. She asked us to pray for him . . . she grabbed my hand and we prayed. . . . It was all I could do to keep from crying. . . ." (Jenny)

To gain God's heart for a world at war with him and each other: "This man and this woman had such a profound effect on me. I fully realized and understood the end result of sin. I actually felt their despair. . . ." (Jenne)

"I had a total change of heart for those who live in the world. I've had only bad feelings before but they have been replaced with compassion and hurt for them." (Mark)

To be stretched to do new things for God: "When I heard I could be part of a construction team building a house for missionaries in Brazil, I was willing but doubted that I could contribute much more than cleaning up. I quickly learned that with good direction, the right attitude, and determination, one can do almost anything." (Megan)

To experience God's power: "I learned that I can do anything with the power of God with me." (Ezra)

"God can do miracles today. We were painting a two-story house and one person was painting at the peak. He was up there for over an hour. When he finished and we took the ladder down we realized the ladder wasn't latched. It should have fallen once he stepped on the extension." (Jewel)

To help others make a step toward God: "We talked with a guy who walked up to us. He was searching many different

Better to Know *Before* You Go

Remember how long it took before your parents let you cross the street by yourself? Imagine the sweat they'll break when you tell them you want to criss-cross the globe. Their little baby needs a passport—not to mention some shots they didn't give you when you were a newborn.

The list below provides some smart questions to ask before you sign up for any short-term project. Some of these are parent-type questions. Humor your parents and face up to four bits of truth. *Fact 1*: You won't go if your parents' questions aren't answered. *Fact 2*: They only want what's best for you. *Fact 3*: Your parents have been around the block a few times, even if they haven't been to the far side of the planet. *Fact 4*: Every other parent is wondering the same things. Calm down.

So here are some things to know before you go:

1. *Who is leading the group?* (As in *How long have they been around? What experience do they have?*) Whether or not you go probably depends on this. Parents don't like youth leaders who use, lose, or abuse kids.

2. *Who can I talk to who's gone before?* Firsthand info. Good stuff. Unless they went with a cult and had their brains washed and wrung dry.

3. *What do they believe?* Does the group fit your background? You might be stretched by going with a different brand of Christians. Then again, you just might snap.

4. *What will I do? How long will I go?* Will you make a real contribution with a measurable end? It's okay to go with what sounds appealing. But stretch beyond that with a project that has a variety of tasks. And make sure it's a world-changing assignment, one that demonstrates God's Good News in both word and

action. Your goal is to make a difference, not perfect your tan.

5. *What's the typical daily schedule?* How many hours will you work each day? What fun stuff do you get to do? Beware of ads, videos, and promotional presentations that look like thumped-up Mountain Dew commercials. Nothing wrong with fun. But you want to work hard and grow much. Look for fun you can't get at home—things you can tell your kids about: seeing cultural sights and unusual scenery, sniffing around local markets, sharing a swimming hole with an alligator.

6. *Where will we stay and what will we eat?* Simple isn't deprivation. Simple is good. You'll find out how little you really need to live.

7. *What rules do they expect me to follow?* Some groups seem tough. It beats going home with a case of lifelong diarrhea or getting shipped home in a box. Don't mess with groups that don't take your safety seriously.

8. *What does it cost? How do I pay?* Does the group have better ways to raise support than bikini car washes?

9. *Do they link us up with local Christians?* You want to know that what you do will be followed up—that it will last.

10. *What do they do to get me ready?* Stay away from groups that don't take preparation seriously. You need to know the ground rules for your time together—what's okay, what's not. One thing is sure: *tough training/easy trip* beats *easy training/tough trip.*

11. *What do they do to get me ready to go home?* It's a cliché to say that a mission trip is a "mountaintop experience" and you need to be prepared for the "valleys" at home. But it's a cliché because it's true. When you run you need to warm up. You need to cool down. Or sooner or later you die.

religions and didn't really research any of them. We explained God's Plan and gave him a Four Spiritual Laws tract. He seemed interested but he really just wanted something for himself other than Christ." (Kevin)

To feel the opposition Christian brothers and sisters feel around the world: "We met a Muslim man named Sahead. He immediately attacked our materials as 'propaganda.' Most of the time he talked about how the Islamic faith and the Koran were the completion of truth, but when we shared things with him that he couldn't explain with Islam he would interrupt. . . . I know we disturbed his idea of 'truth.' " (Kierstenmarie)

To understand prayer/depend on God: "This was the first time I fully realized the incredible power of group prayer. Things went so well that it had to have been God intervening in our work. People mostly got along, we got a ton of work done, and chances to witness kept popping up everywhere. . . . This camp really taught me to put my trust in God, and to look at him as a great provider." (Jessie)

To learn humility: "I learned to humble myself before God. Sometimes it's hard to get out there and sweat and do work that I'd rather not be doing. But God tells us to be servants of all, and when we humble ourselves he will lift us up." (Elissa)

To learn to work together: "I really learned what teamwork means. Sometimes I wanted total credit for all the work *I* was doing, so I wanted to do it all by myself. But I learned that I was doing everything for God and all the credit was for him. By letting others help me the job gets done better." (Elissa)

To learn God's care as you express God's care: "God has helped me get through many tough times. I know that he is the only one who will *always* be there for me. I have also learned that God has a plan for me, and that if I give everything over to him his will for my life will be done." (Kelly)

Finding Your Way From Here to There

You may already know of groups and programs that give you the chance to serve far away or in a city or rural area nearby. Some may be run by your church. Others may be run by groups your church works with often.

The groups you know are great places to start. You know who you're going with, what you'll do, and what the experience will be like. Your pastor probably knows of opportunities with urban ministries, county or regional outreaches in your area, or camps where you can serve. If your church belongs to a denomination, they probably run programs.

Your own youth group may run projects you can join. It's great because you know the program, but because you know the program it may not be fresh for you or for the leaders, who may have led the same trip year after year. Big advantage: You know the people you're going with. Big disadvantage: You know the people you're going with.

You can sign up with an organization that takes individual teens. You'll go with teens you don't know—like Erica in chapter 7. Some ups and downs: You can get away from it all. You can reinvent yourself. You make friends from all over the country. You nearly die when you have to say good-bye. You can also sign up and go with a friend or two—although the group is likely to frown on your friendship if it gets in the way of the group working together. Check "Stuff at the Back of the Book" for a Web site listing some of the organizations that serve teens in North America.

Some groups allow you to go with your family. Great time! The trips tend to be shorter, though, because sooner or later your parents have to go back to work.

There's one other opportunity—if you're up to it. *You can go on an exchange program* as a high school or college student. Think 6 Ls: It's *long-term*, usually at least a semester. The focus is on academic and cultural *learning*. Whenever you go there are *losses*, things you'll miss out on back home. Exchange programs can attract a lot of *loonies* searching for who knows what—though you don't have to be one to go! Going is almost always—at times—incredibly *lonely*. But it's also a *lotta lotta fun*. Check with your school and church for organizations you can go with. If you're serious about going get serious about finding a church to worship at *before* you go.

Are You Ready?

A short-term mission trip can be a great way to catch *The Wave*. But think hard about these questions. They aren't meant to spoil the ride but to help you make the most of it:

1. *Why am I going?* If you've read this far you understand God's plan for the planet. Looking for adventure is part of how God wires human beings, but you need a higher motivation than going just to shop or sightsee. Are you truly interested in enlarging God's people?

2. *What am I doing to be spiritually prepared?* For most groups you can be a baby Christian. But do you want to grow up? What are you doing at home to help that happen?

3. *What can I contribute to the work?* The important answer here is "I will do my best at anything."

4. *Am I willing to follow rules and work as a team?* Don't get in the way of what others want to do!

5. *What can I do to thank the people who support me with prayer and money?* A trip is a big investment. People don't mind the cost as long as their investment pays off.

If you go on a trip with the wrong mindset—and the trip doesn't change that—you'll come home with a bored attitude of "been there, done that." But you're far more likely to have your life turned upside down. This is what one adult wrote to the group who took him for a summer as a teen:

> I had left home wanting more. I found *Him*—Christ. I found *them*—Christian brothers and sisters. I found *it*—a new life. What I learned upended my goals and priorities. . . . If I had gone home that summer empty-handed I would have kept looking for something better to live for, some person or idea or cause bigger than the God I had known. But because you take teens, their need for Christ, and God's ability to use them seriously, it was Christ that I found afresh. I found that my Savior wants and deserves my life, and calls me to share Him with others.
>
> WaveCatcher for life!

But in your hearts set apart Christ as

Lord. Always be prepared to give an

answer to everyone who asks you to

give the reason for the hope that

you have. But do this with gentleness

and respect.

—1 Peter 3:15

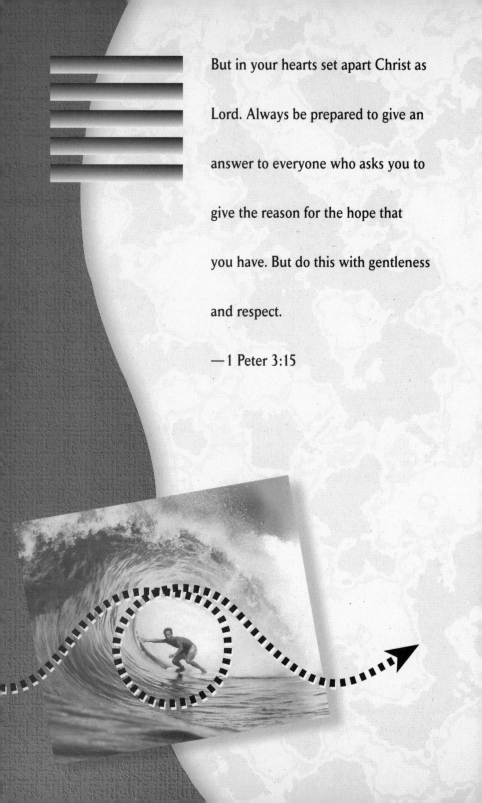

10

Lifeguard Duty

"I need a break," Nikki moaned as she fake-collapsed in the middle of a thrashing backyard volleyball game. When her team dragged her from the court she brushed herself off and headed inside to check on the other half of the party. In a quiet corner of the living room a guy and a girl sat off by themselves. No liplocking going on—Nikki heard the girl telling the guy how she became a Christian. Five or six others sat around a couple guys jamming worship songs on a guitar. Then there was the huddle in the dining room praying with a friend as she received Christ.

Not your average high school party.

Nothing had been very average since Nikki's church got a new youth pastor—a fiery Christian with a bushy blond hairdo and a wild guitar. To John, God wasn't a figment of cranky church ladies' imaginations. God had invaded John's life—a total transmogrification. When teens saw life through John's eyes they caught a vision of God's glory. Within a couple of years John's group grew from ten stone-cold teens to more than a hundred who'd decided to follow Christ. Shy girls, theatrical guys, jocks, eggheads—when they burst out on their world, they couldn't help but talk about God.

Talking Up Your Faith

Whenever you show love for God and the world he's made, you demonstrate what God has done for you—and what he wants to do for others. God's Good News is something you *live*. But it's also something you *say*:

> "Go, stand in the temple courts," [an angel of the Lord] said, "and tell the people the full message of this new life."
>
> Acts 5:20

> We are therefore Christ's ambassadors, as though God were making his appeal through us. We implore you on Christ's behalf: Be reconciled to God.
>
> 2 Corinthians 5:20

> But in your hearts set apart Christ as Lord. Always be prepared to give an answer to everyone who asks you to give the reason for the hope that you have. But do this with gentleness and respect.
>
> 1 Peter 3:15

You might be able to muscle your way through life and *do* what's right—performing impressive feats with your faith, working hard to treat people the way God treats you, opposing the crowd when you need to. But *talk* about what you believe? That might be tougher.

Get the News Out

Paul said that "faith comes from hearing the message, and the message is heard through the word of Christ" (Romans 10:17). There's no way around it: People can't hear about Christ and chase after him if you don't split your lips and speak up. But what should you say?

That's a problem.

Suppose you're a guy in love with the most beauteous girl ever. You're totally gone. It's a godly relationship with an authentic woman of God. So how would you explain that to others? You could say what she's like—rattle off her shoe size, her mother's maiden name, and what kind of cat her dog likes to eat. You could say how she makes your heart rumble. Or you could explain how you found her. Too much to say!

It's the same with God. There's so much to tell. Every bit of it sheds light on God. Your friends—whether they're friends here, there, or anywhere—need to know *who God is*. That he's Ultimate Power, Ultimate Intelligence, Ultimate Justice, and Ultimate Love. It's persuasive if they grasp *what he's done for you*. But somewhere along the way they need to get their facts straight. They need to know *how they can have a relationship with God*.

That's what you want to get in their heads. They need to get a hold on three simple facts of life.

~~~

Fact of Life #1

There's a PROBLEM between us and God: sin.

~~~

God knows right. He thinks, feels, and does right—perfectly. We don't. We sin in the bad we do. We sin in the good we don't do. Sin is more than listening to kill-your-mother music or watching naked-people movies. The Bible's roll call of sins and sinners nails all of us: Exodus says *Have no false gods. Don't treat God's name with disrespect. Worship God only. Honor Mom and Dad. Don't murder, sleep around, steal, lie,* or *wish you could* (Exodus 20:1–17). Paul lists *witchcraft, drunkenness, hatred, strife, jealousy, rage, selfish ambition, quarrels* (Galatians 5:19–21). In another spot he includes *greed, bitterness, impurity, sexual wrong, slander, obscenity, dirty jokes* (Ephesians 4:31—5:5). And Jesus points out that you don't have to *do* those things to be in the wrong—sins of the heart are just as dark (Matthew 5:28).

Don't poke at your friends and say *they* are sinners. The truth is that we are *all* sinners: "All have sinned and fall short of the glory of God" (Romans 3:23).

Fact of Life #2

God has a SOLUTION to our problem: Christ's death for us on the cross.

"The wages of sin is death," the Bible says, "but the gift of God is eternal life in Christ Jesus our Lord" (Romans 6:23). God doesn't shrug off sin. Sin erects a wall between us and God—permanent separation from him. It's a pain and loneliness that starts now and worsens for eternity.

But we don't have to stay far from God. God's penalty for sin is death, yet God's Good News is that Jesus paid the penalty for us. He died a death he didn't deserve. On the cross his agony demonstrated the awfulness of sin for all time. And he bore God's total anger toward a sinful human race.

Fact of Life #3

God expects our RESPONSE: He wants us to receive him—to change our minds about sin and about him.

Our response is to accept God's solution—to trust in who Jesus is and what he accomplished for us. These are the terms of the friendship he offers: "To all who received him, to those who believed in his name, he gave the right to become children of God" (John 1:12). *To receive him means we change our minds about sin.* God doesn't want us just sorry that his cosmic X-ray vision spotted us sneaky little evil-doers—sorry we got caught. He wants us to comprehend through and through the hurt we caused ourselves, others, and him. And he wants us to understand the wrongness of our wrong. *To receive him means we change our minds about God.* We finally admit that God is on our side. That his commands are wholly good, totally kind. That his gift of forgiveness is the one way our sins can be wiped away so we can be accepted by him.

Receiving Christ might happen in a prayer we can pinpoint in time and space: "God, I know I've sinned against you. Thank you that Christ died in my place and took the punishment I deserved. Thank you for forgiving me. Help me to follow you." Or receiving him might be an attitude of trust and faith that grows over time. Either way, the result is the same: we start a new life lived as God's friend.

Colossians ties together these three facts in one spot. These verses are definitely worth sticking in your brain:

PROBLEM: At one time you were separated from God. You were enemies in your minds, and the evil things you did were against God.

SOLUTION: But now God has made you his friends again. He did this through Christ's death in the body so that he might bring you into God's presence as people who are holy, with no wrong, and with nothing of which God can judge you guilty.

RESPONSE: This will happen if you continue strong and sure in your faith. You must not be moved away from the hope brought to you by the Good News that you heard (Colossians 1:21–23, NCV).

Problem, solution, response—those are the three facts of life your friends need to know.

Tough Sell

Here's the hard part. You might be surrounded by friends who nod "yes" to those three facts. They say they're

Christians—but they sure don't look like it from the outside. Remember from chapter 4 what a "nominal Christian" is? It's someone who is a Christian in name only, whose claim to Christianity depends more on *church*ianity or *culture* or *family* than on a life-changing grasp of God's plan.

If you were put in a room with six live people and six dead people, you wouldn't have a hard time telling which was which. Sure, from across the room you might mistakenly think someone was snoozing—and there are tragic cases where only God knows whether a person still lives inside the shell of a comatose body. But you can usually distinguish dead bodies from live ones.

Christians are spiritually alive. They're the ones who are moving. Growing. Non-Christians are spiritually dead. Now you only see their outsides. You can't peer into their guts for positive proof their faith is or isn't even a little bit alive. Only God can. But their lack of vital signs makes you suspicious. As you talk with the friends you worry about you can fill them in little by little on what the Bible says a real Christian looks like:

- ➤ Real Christians are *reconciled*—they've become friends with God: "Therefore, since we have been justified through faith, we have peace with God through our Lord Jesus Christ, through whom we have gained access by faith into this grace in which we now stand" (Romans 5:1).
- ➤ Real Christians are *rescued*—they're owned by God: "For he has rescued us from the dominion of darkness and brought us into the kingdom of the Son he loves, in whom we have redemption, the forgiveness of sins" (Colossians 1:13–14).
- ➤ Real Christians are *under reconstruction*—they're being changed from the inside out by God: "For the grace of God that brings salvation has appeared to all men. It teaches us to say "No" to ungodliness and worldly passions, and to live self-controlled, upright and godly lives . . . eager to do what is good" (Titus 2:11–12, 14).

- ☞ Real Christians are *responsive*—they're listening for God's commands and carrying them out: "We know that we have come to know him if we obey his commands. . . . This is how we know we are in him: Whoever claims to live in him must walk as Jesus did" (1 John 2:3, 5b–6).
- ☞ Real Christians are *resilient*—they get up and go on after they mess up: "If we claim to be without sin, we deceive ourselves and the truth is not in us. If we confess our sins, he is faithful and just and will forgive us our sins and purify us from all unrighteousness" (1 John 1:8–9).

Scripture is like a mirror. You can hold it up to your friends and they can gaze at their true selves. Do they see anything real? Or are they vampires—dressed to kill but actually dead, reflecting nothing in the mirror? Some of the people you talk to may realize they're stuck in spiritual babyhood. They started in a relationship with God, but now they need to grow up. Others will realize they've never even made the first step. Either way, you and the other Christians around you can help them take their next step.

They Still Aren't Buying It

Even when you bust loose and tell people about Christ, they don't always listen. To everything you say they throw up objection after objection. Most people you'll meet, though, who say they disagree with the truths of Christianity don't know the Bible they're arguing with. Let the Bible speak for itself. Here are a few of the prime arguments you'll hear and some verses to politely point to:

1. *Believing in God is for wimps* (2 Corinthians 11:23–27—Read Paul's diary. He wasn't exactly a wuss).

2. *Christianity is fine for you. But there are a lot of other good religions. Jesus was just another teacher* (John 14:6—Jesus himself claimed to be the only way).

3. *God is fine. I hate church. It's a bore and I don't need it* (Hebrews 10:23–25—We need each other to get strong).

4. *Why should I listen to you? Christians are hypocrites—they always say one thing and do another* (Isaiah 29:13–14—God gets disgusted with hypocrites more than we ever will).

5. *God loves everyone. He wouldn't send anyone to hell* (Psalm 14:1–3; Romans 3:23, 6:23—God will judge each of us whether we think he will or not).

6. *Science proves the Bible isn't true* or *The Bible is full of myths. Why should I believe it?* (2 Timothy 2:16—Ask them to name specific myths or points where science contradicts the Bible. Often they can't offer any.)

7. *God doesn't exist. I've never gotten an answer when I've prayed* (Psalm 14:1; James 4:3—God's reality isn't limited to our knowledge of him).

You don't have to rely on your own brainpower and Bible knowledge to answer people who argue with you. There's no such thing as a new spiritual question. Check out unbeatable books like these to help answer tough questions and to know more about how to spread God's News:

- *If I Could Ask God One Question* (Greg Johnson)
- *Keeping Your Cool While Sharing Your Faith* (Greg Johnson and Susie Shellenberger)
- *Geek Proof Your Faith* (Greg Johnson and Michael Ross)
- *Don't Check Your Brains at the Door* (Josh McDowell and Bob Hostetler).
- *Evidence That Demands a Verdict* (Josh McDowell).

God's News is something you *live*. But it's also something you *say*.

Keep at the task. But hang on to your head. It isn't your job to jab your finger up the noses of your non-Christian friends. The Good News isn't your message. It's God's message. You don't do the fixing. God does. True, you speak the News. But God draws people to himself.

"Remember that God does the converting, not you," Lindsey wrote to some friends headed overseas to spread

God's News. "You're only his tool. If someone rejects you, know that this must not be his time. If you think you messed up or think of something to say later on, remember that God can use you and work through you no matter what."

I am the vine; you are the branches.

If a man remains in me and I in him,

he will bear much fruit; apart from me

you can do nothing.

—John 15:5

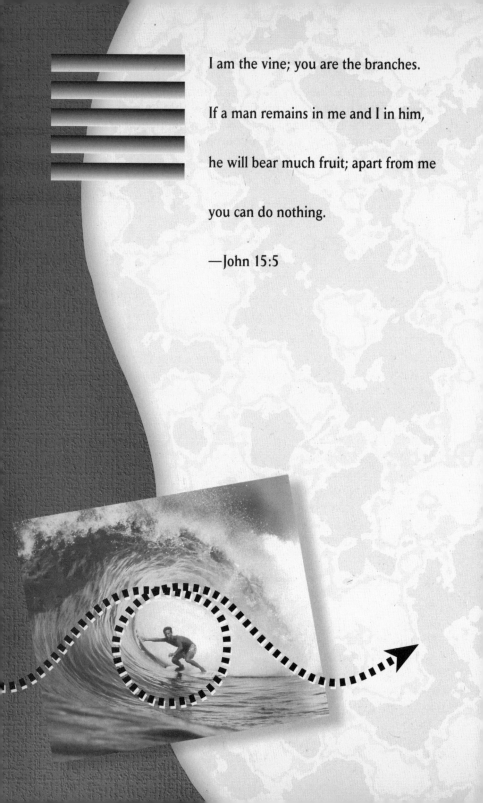

11

Waxing Your Board

"Jackie can't breathe!" Sarah screamed. Their teammates looked up from their construction work to see Jackie standing motionless under the broiling South American sun. Hands at her throat, Jackie gasped for breath as if someone were strangling her. Ten of her teammates rushed to gather around her. Even if everyone had been back home they would have wondered what to do. No call to 911 could get help fast enough. And here?

"Pray!" someone cried. For a couple minutes Jackie's teammates struggled to stay calm, watching her wheeze and hoping her throat wouldn't clamp up even more. They prayed. They begged God for the help only he could give.

Suddenly the spasm in Jackie's throat stopped.

Hanging Tight

You won't catch *The Wave* if you never learn how to rely on Jesus. And you can't reach your world if you wander away from him.

You miss your chance to catch *The Wave* when you don't *obey* Jesus. Sheila debated her social studies teacher her whole senior year. She told him she disagreed with his beliefs about abortion and homosexuality. She fussed when he made the class read a trashy novel for its "cultural content."

So when Sheila ditched class on an outlawed senior skip day her teacher was less than wowed. How she acted didn't match what she claimed to stand for—and her teacher filed that in a drawer in his brain labeled "Reasons why I'm not a Christian."

You miss your chance to catch *The Wave* when you don't *depend on* Jesus. Some days Sheila attempted to change her world all on her own. She left no time or space for God to tug people to himself. She plugged her ears and set her mouth to auto-detonate, attacking her pagan classmates without trying to understand them.

You can work hard to do all the right things to show and tell God's Good News. But you'll fail miserably if you forget what Jesus said: the only way that you can impact your world is by relying on him: "I am the vine; you are the branches. If a man remains in me and I in him, he will bear much fruit; apart from me you can do nothing" (John 15:5).

When Jesus says "remain" he isn't talking about the long-division contortions you learned in elementary school. By reminding you of your need for him Jesus isn't trying to put you down. He just wants you to know without a doubt that disconnected from him you'll wither and die—like a branch chainsawed from the trunk of a tree. You can't obey without his help. You won't show signs of life if you're not connected to your source of life. All the effort you pour into spreading God's News will fizzle if the power doesn't come from God.

So how do you depend on Jesus? There are three ways to hang tight with him: by remembering you're not boss of your life, by letting God fill you with his power, and by praying and admitting to God you need him.

Who's Your Boss?

God has big plans for you. But his big plans leave no room for a big head. When you're part of what God is doing around the world you can start to feel like a superhero—crusading for peace, justice, and the Jesus way. You ponder getting your own comic book. You wonder when a toy company will take your measurements and photograph your face and make you into a six-inch injection-molded action figure with special halt-the-evildoers action. You'd be a hit, you think.

Don't morph just yet. God only sent one hero to the planet—Jesus. Your job is to draw attention to him, not to yourself. Think about this and be wise: God can replace you with a rock whenever he wants (Luke 19:40).

If anyone had a claim to a lavish welcome as God's messenger, it was Jesus himself. He was God in human flesh. He deserved earsplitting praise, rich accommodations, one-of-a kind recognition.

That wasn't the path he chose. He told his followers, in fact, that he "did not come to be served, but to serve, and to give his life as a ransom for many" (Matthew 20:28). If we were him we'd expect to soak in a hot-tubbed limo. He came expecting a carry-and-wear cross.

Remembering who's in charge means you go into your world as a servant. Listen to what Paul wrote: "Your attitude should be the same as that of Christ Jesus: Who, being in very nature God, did not consider equality with God something to be grasped, but made himself nothing, taking the very nature of a servant . . . he humbled himself and became obedient to death—even death on a cross!" (Philippians 2:5–8).

Only Jesus could die on the cross. But you have the opportunity in all you do to be a servant—to sacrifice for the sake of others. "Serving and being humble isn't glamorous," Kierstenmarie says about her summer mission trip. "Sometimes it means you don't get a shower and you look worse than everyone else all day because of it. Sometimes it means being last in line or pushed around. But I learned it doesn't matter. That's it—it just doesn't matter."

Remembering who's in charge means you go to your world as a learner. Other members of God's family will teach you lessons you can't afford to miss. And even non-Christian people and cultures can teach you more than a thing or two. Megan is a high school senior working with elementary school girls at her church. "I have been encouraged by the faith of some of these girls," she says. "I know that some spend a lot of quiet time with the Lord and share God openly with their friends. These girls especially bring me a lot of joy."

Remembering who's in charge means you go into your world to love the less-than-lovable. Whether you're at church, school, or anywhere else, look around for people on the outside looking in. You may be the difference between heaven and hell for that kid—whether he senses God's love or feels mistreated by the church too. Thad counseled church kids and their friends at a summer camp: "I learned that a little bit of love goes a long way. Some of the nerdy kids at camp came out of their shells when I just talked to them and joked with them. It was cool, because I got to be a witness and make a new friend."

Powerboarding

You can tell people here, there, and everywhere about Jesus. You can explain what the Bible says about what it means to be a Christian. You can show God's love by being a servant. But it's not enough for people to hear about Christ—even to see him living in you. They need to understand and act on what they hear—to receive and follow. That won't happen without God's working inside them. "No one can come to me," Jesus said, "unless the Father who sent me draws him" (John 6:44).

You'll go nuts if you think you can mutate people and make them follow Christ. You'll get pushy and ugly and try to hijack God's job. It's the Holy Spirit who does the real work inside the people you talk to. He "testifies" to Christ, making real everything you explain (John 15:26). He convinces people of the wrongness of their sin, of God's powerful goodness, and Christ's defeat of Satan (John 16:7–11).

The Holy Spirit also works in *you*, giving you power to boldly show and say who Christ is (Acts 1:8). "I really could feel the Spirit of God take away my fears and work through me!" Karen said about her experience on a trip overseas. "As I handed out flyers I began to feel love and compassion for the people we passed even though I knew none of them! I only pray that God will use me in such ways again!"

God powers you up every time you study the Bible or learn from other Christians. The Holy Spirit also makes you achieve things beyond anything you could normally do, through the gifts mentioned in chapter 7. Believers disagree on the kinds of supernatural power displays God does today—things like healings, miracles, tongues, prophecies— but almost everyone agrees that God is able to do whatever he wants whenever he wants. Don't underestimate God in action!

God's Holy Spirit is with the people you talk to before you get to them. He'll be there after you leave. Besides that, he's working inside of you. Depending on God means you're doing the things this book has talked about—then leaving the fixing to God.

Coming Up for Air

Prayer is like breathing. You'd better *do it all the time*, but at times you need to *stop and think about it*. Prayer is an attitude that lasts all day, but there are times when you want to settle down long enough to just pray.

Whatever you're trying to do to build God's people here, there, or anywhere, prayer is where you start. God gives us some major reasons to pray:

You can pray and tell God you want what he wants. If God is the one you've put in charge of your life—and if he's the one who powers all you do—it's a good idea to tell him you're ready to get to work. Telling God you want to do his will is part of the Bible's simplest prayer—the one Jesus taught his disciples: "Your kingdom come," he told us to pray, "your will be done on earth as it is in heaven" (Matthew 6:10). It's part of the Bible's most gut-churning prayer—the one Jesus prayed just before going to the cross. Jesus told his Father, "May your will be done" (Matthew 26:42). Depending on God begins and ends with telling God you want what he wants.

You can pray and tell God how great he is. You can't ignore God's goodness—his total power, total intelligence, total justice, and total love. You don't have to keep quiet about it. Check out Psalm 150:1–2. It says *what* to praise him for: "Praise the LORD. Praise God in his sanctuary; praise him in his mighty heavens. Praise him for his acts of power; praise him for his surpassing greatness." The rest of Psalm 150 tells *how* to praise him: with trumpet, harp, tambourine, dancing, strings, flute, the clash of cymbals—and with every breath.

You can pray and invite God to break through and change the world. It would be fine with you if God started with your English essay—by writing it for you. Or when you're facing a 3–2 count you wouldn't mind his help with hitting a home run. God would miss the chance to chat if you stopped praying those panic prayers for tests and teachers and touchdowns. But God also wants you to ask him to act on things that matter even more. Like what? You can ask that more people would catch *The Wave*. For *the people you talk with to be willing to listen.* For *Christians to get along so that the world recognizes Christ in us* (John 17:23). For *a bigger view of God.*

You can ask God to meet needs all around you. You have some. So do your family, friends, city, state, country, and world. Prayer lets you reach out and touch someone down the block or next to you at school—or on the far side of the planet.

Prayer That Works

If you want to meet a friend at the mall you've got to get your heads together. You need a spot. You set a time. If you mess up the message you'll both stand around looking stupid. The same thing goes for prayer. You have to *plan* to pray.

Pray with friends. Take time to pray alone. But when you pray for big needs and tough needs it helps to pray with a big tough group.

Pray for solid stuff. You'll never notice answers to fuzzy prayers like "God bless my school." The only way you'll spot God's response is if you make specific requests.

Stay alert. Your church, your youth group, your friends, and missionaries can all stir your brain with things to pray about. Patrick Johnstone's *Operation World* and materials

from the AD2000 & Beyond Movement help you pray for
the world.

Go With God

When Jesus sends you out to your world to spread his
News he doesn't kick you out by your lonesome. He said
this: Make disciples of all nations. Baptize them in the name
of the Father, Son, and Holy Spirit. Teach them to obey him.
And then he says this: "And surely I am with you always,
to the very end of the age" (Matthew 28:20).

If you could change the world by yourself, Jesus could
have stayed home. God could sleep in. But instead he's with
you. Depend on it.

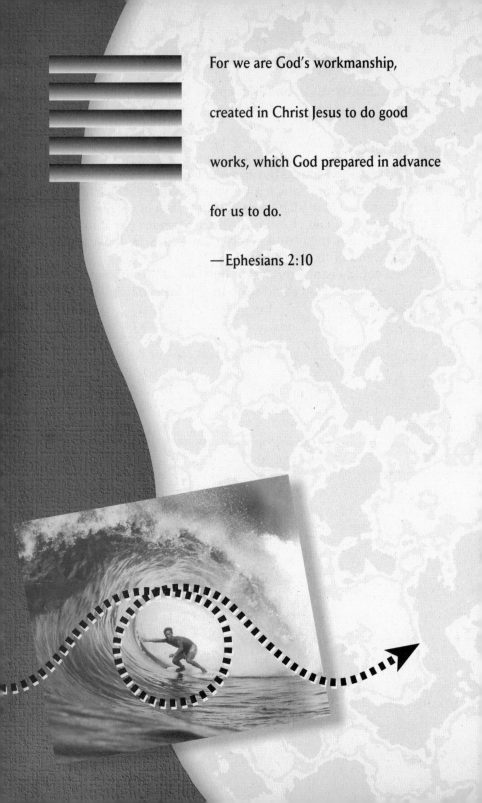

For we are God's workmanship,

created in Christ Jesus to do good

works, which God prepared in advance

for us to do.

—Ephesians 2:10

12

Becoming One With *The Wave*

You're sure of two things. *One*: You know God has a mammoth plan to build a group of friends who belong to him—a tight group formed from every people on earth. And *two*: You know there's a place for you in his plan.

But *where*?

Your spot could be here, there, or anywhere. That's the problem. You're trying hard to follow God. You've begun to figure out how to catch *The Wave* at school and inside and outside of church. You hear of more and more chances to go places short-term. You're *here* right now. You can go *there* and *everywhere* sometimes. But what about later—like when you're done with high school or college? Chapter 6 showed you six no-brainer things you can do to be part of God's people-building plan. When you belong to God you can be sure that you're a *Follower* . . . an *Example* . . . a *Witness* . . . a *Prayer Warrior* . . . a *Sender* . . . and maybe a *Goer*.

It's the last one that's tougher to figure out—the *maybe* part. Especially when you think about being a *Goer* long-term. Not just for a summer or a Christmas break, but for a chunk of your lifetime.

You maybe wonder whether God wants you to be a long-term Goer—a career missionary.

Fact 1: Most missionaries say that they first felt God prodding them toward the mission field when they were between the ages of 12 and 14.

Fact 2: Ninety percent of teens who sense that call to the mission field change their mind by the time they enter college (USCWM—cited in Azusa Pacific University *Conquest '96 literature*).

So here's the truth: You're not too young to wonder. Even to feel strongly tugged to missions. But the numbers say your next few years could be confusing.

Finding the Perfect Wave

So how do you know what God wants from you in the future? Does he want you to be a missionary?

Bad news: No one can answer that for you.

Good news: God has given you some ways to help you know what he wants. Before we look at *how* you can know, we need to look at *how much* you can know. Let's look at four assumptions from the Bible:

WaveCatcher's Rule #1

Your commitment to do what God wants needs to be total.

God made you. He's King. Like everyone else, you fled his rule. But when you accepted God's forgiveness you admitted you'd been wrong. Bit by bit you quit your rebellion, and you're learning to submit to his rule. Paul puts it this way: "For Christ's love compels us, because we are convinced that one died for all, and therefore all died. And he died for all, that those who live should no longer live for themselves but for him who died for them and was raised again" (2 Corinthians 5:14–15). You love God. Your life belongs to him. What he says, you seek to do.

WaveCatcher's Rule #2

Your understanding of what God wants may be incomplete.

Picture this: You're driving on a country road on a moonless night. Your headlights brighten the road *one hundred* feet in front of you. But you're driving fast enough that even if you slammed on the brakes it would take *two hundred* feet to stop. You can't see as far ahead as you need to. That's called "overdriving your headlights." It's scary. You're cheese spread if a deer leaps in front of you. You could plunge stupidly into the darkness. Or you could slow down.

You probably want to drive your Christian life with your foot to the floor. To push forward. For God to tell you exactly what your future holds and to get there fast.

You have to slow down. You have to stick to God's speed limit.

Just because you *want* to do what's right doesn't mean you will always *know* what's right. In the Bible God makes clear 99 percent of what he wants you to do—and not do. But when it comes to showing you your future he usually leaves things a little hazy. God doesn't often give you the details and the foresight you'd like way ahead of time—who you're going to marry, where you're going to live, how many bambinos you'll bear, what exact job you'll have.

Here's why: God wants you to walk with him *step by step*—and if he told all today you wouldn't need him tomorrow. James states the rule: "Now listen, you who say, 'Today or tomorrow we will go to this or that city, spend a year there, carry on business and make money.' Why, you do not even know what will happen tomorrow. What is your life? You are a mist that appears for a little while and then vanishes. Instead, you ought to say, 'If it is the Lord's will, we will live and do this or that'" (James 4:13–15). True vision from God always comes mixed with a healthy dose of humility toward your ability to peer into the future. And of a minute-by-minute dependence on him.

Sure, God can make exceptions to his rule. He may have flashed the high beams of life so far into your future that you're certain of when and where and how you should serve him. But you still have to get there from here—you'll have to test what you believe is God's guidance to make sure it was him you heard. And just because you think you *haven't* heard God say "Git!" doesn't mean he won't. You don't have to feel guilty or fake a "call" because all your friends say God spoke to them to head for the mission field. God may just be waiting to show you later.

WaveCatcher's Rule #3

You can't assume EVERYONE is a Goer.

Some people say that unless God yells at you to stay home you'd better go someplace far away to spread God's Good News. It's an idea usually built on a skewed view that being a career missionary is the only real job in God's kingdom.

What we're involved in is like a war. Some soldiers and civilians stay home building lunch boxes, bombs, and bazookas. Other soldiers are holding ground that's been won and are transporting supplies. And still others are on the front lines, battling to capture enemy territory. When we finally win the war, who did the winning? Everyone everywhere who did his or her part. When the church does its job and reaches unreached peoples, who did the work? Everyone everywhere who did his or her part.

No bombs, please. God works by persuasion, not force.

But here's the point: No job is worth any less to the ultimate goal.

God gives us different gifts and different roles (Romans 12:6–8; 1 Corinthians 12–14; Ephesians 4:12–16). In missionary terms, some are *Goers*—the ones on the front lines. Some are *Senders*—people who stay home, pay the bills, and pray. Some are *Welcomers*—people who take care of the millions of unreached peoples who wander our way as students, businesspeople, or immigrants. Some are *Mobilizers*—people who encourage and equip the rest of us. Without people in each role our efforts will fail.

WaveCatcher's Rule #4

It's wrong to assume you're NOT a Goer.

The fact that God could want you to serve long-term in another culture might be the last thing you want to hear. *Strange food. Bizarre languages. Bulging crowds—or no one for miles. So far from home.* You might want to duck like you do when your math teacher wants a volunteer to work at the board.

God *is* Master. He has the right at any time and in any way to ask you to serve in any place he wills. " 'Come, follow me,' Jesus said, 'and I will make you fishers of men' " (Matthew 4:19). When in doubt of Jesus' lordship refer to WaveCatcher's Rule #1! But don't crawl under your desk just yet. What God asks you to do he gives you strength to do.

The choices you make in the next few years will shape how you spend the rest of your life. As you mull careers and life directions don't ever shortchange God or yourself by ruling out the possibility that you may have a full-time place in God's plan. Here's why. . . .

Getting There From Here

Nowhere in the Bible does it say you have to feel a melodramatic "call from God" to become a worker among the peoples of the world. In fact, the steps you can take to get there from here don't have to be mysterious at all. Whether or not you think right now that God wants you to be a Goer, it's possible to find out whether the mission field is the place for you.

Step One: Surrender Your Heart

Be willing! It's the step you have to take before you take any of the others. Did you declare "I Want to Catch *The Wave!*" back in chapter 5? That's the starting point. Admit that your whole life and your total obedience belong to God. Agree that spreading God's Good News is utterly important. Promise to stick close to God and find whatever role he has for you wherever he leads. Surrendering your heart means you give all of yourself to God (Romans 12:1–2).

Step Two: Speak Up

God is happy to guide you—be aware, though, that he usually leads one step at a time, keeping you close to him and checking your obedience. But *God wants you to ask him to show you what he wants*: "If any of you lacks wisdom, he should ask God, who gives generously to all without finding fault, and it will be given to him" (James 1:5).

God never blames you for not knowing. What he despises is "double-mindedness." He wants you to be sure of his care and sure that you intend to do what he says. If you waver between wanting what *God* wants and wanting to hear what *you* want, God isn't likely to give you the guidance you're only sort-of asking for (James 1:7). Speaking up means you tell God you want to know what he wants.

Step Three: Clean Out Your Ears

James says another smart thing. He says you're silly if you get up in the morning, study yourself in the bathroom mirror, and then go away without fixing your face and brushing away your morning breath. God means for you to develop your ability to hear and do something about his words. He guides you through the *Bible*—his clear-cut, no-way-around-them commands. Anything crucial he has made clear. He also guides you through *conviction*, making you sure of what's right as you offer yourself to him (Romans 12:2). Cleaning out your ears means you obey what you hear: "Do not merely listen to the word, and so deceive yourselves. Do what it says" (James 1:22).

Step Four: Study Your Innards

God doesn't drop different gifts on Christians for no reason. He says that the variety is every bit as necessary to the work of the church as the variety of your body parts is to the functioning of your bodies. The gifts are given "to prepare God's people for works of service" (Ephesians 4:12). You need to figure out what God has wired you to do.

It's great to want to be "a missionary." But there's no such thing as a one-size-fits-all missionary. You have to *do* something. And what you do depends on the mix between your spiritual gifts (like those listed throughout the Bible) and your natural gifts (your talents). In chapter 9 you saw the list of what teens have done in short-term missions. Those are just a smidgen of what you can do as a trained career missionary. Practically any career skill you can think of is a tool you can use as a missionary to enlarge God's people!

You need balance here. *You need to develop your natural gifts.* As a missionary you need a way to provide for yourself during the years you'll spend in your home country. You might prepare to work in the church. Or you may pick out a "secular" job—like agriculture, media, medicine, engineering, linguistics, or teaching. Those skills can be your ticket into countries that ban missionaries—what's called "creative access." You can be a "tentmaker" and work a job in a foreign culture to pay your own way. *But you also need to develop your spiritual gifts* that enable you to evangelize, teach, support, and lead. And here's the trick: *You need to wisely develop both parts of you.* You need to study hard at school *and* do ministry now. You need to get training *but not* get distracted. Not easy. (A book like *Run With the Vision* by Bob Sjogren and Bill and Amy Stearns can tell you how.)

So what are you good at? Get great at it! Studying your innards means finding how God has gifted you and developing those gifts.

Step Five: Keep Your Head Screwed On

Christian speaker Tony Campolo is famous for asking if a Christian can own a BMW. Here's a different angle: Why would you want to? Aren't there more important things in life? As you become an adult it's easy to misplace your head. You see all the possibilities: a big house filled with neat stuff, a hot car, a cushy life. Amid the glitz you forget God's goal for the world. (To be fair, you can also get stuck on being poor. You can be so frugal and so intent on saving money that you also push aside God's plan as well.)

Bad choices make it tough for you to follow God. Fall in love with a non-Christian and you won't make it to the mission field. You won't go anytime soon if you rack up tens of thousands of dollars in college debts.

Again, learn balance. Just don't make choices that make it impossible to be a Goer. Listen to this proverb: "Give me neither poverty nor riches, but give me only my daily bread. Otherwise, I may have too much and disown you and say, 'Who is the LORD?' Or I may become poor and steal, and so dishonor the name of my God" (Proverbs 30:8–9). Keeping your head screwed on means you learn to be content with what you have because God and his purposes for you come first (Philippians 4:11–13).

Step Six: Open Your Eyes

Why share God's News with people you don't care about? Why pray for people you don't love? And why love people you don't know? "For God so loved the world," John wrote, "that he gave his one and only Son, that whoever believes in him shall not perish but have eternal life" (John 3:16). God knows and loves the planet he made.

It's easier than ever to stretch your view of the world. Cable and satellite TV, videos, software, newspapers, books, magazines, the Internet, and worldband radio can all make you a globehead without leaving home. If you've never spent time in another culture, then going on a short-term project to the inner-city or a foreign country will rattle your world. Opening your eyes means you get to know the world God loves.

Step Seven: Make the Connection

You don't have to be sure that you're going to go to take this final step. You don't have to feel God prodding YOU to go to the ends of the earth. Because *making the connection* is where you really test your role in God's plan.

You need to connect with your *peers*. Moving to another culture makes spreading God's News harder, not easier. So don't hide from non-Christians now. At school get involved in team sports and group activities like drama or choir or band or the school newspaper. It's in those settings that you figure out how to relate to other people. You discover what works and what doesn't as you tell others about Christ. You learn to hold your ground as a Christian without being obnoxious. You need to practice now whatever you want to do later.

You need to connect with *patrons*. Back in the Renaissance, wealthy families supported and sheltered painters and architects and scholars. A patron's money and protection allowed the Michelangelos of the time to do their stuff. If you want to catch *The Wave* in another culture you need sturdy support—people who will stand behind you with prayer, encouragement and, at times, financial help. You need, most of all, for your church to back you. Ask your youth pastor or sponsors what key adults in your church— a pastor, elder, missions committee chairperson—could help you figure out God's place in his plan.

You need to connect with *partners*. Only an idiot would

get on a plane bound for China not knowing how to say, "Where's the bathroom?" *Partners* are the people who can train you to work in another world—and who know how to get you there. You'll want to explore the swarm of groups formed to help you—everyone from Bible schools, Christian colleges and universities, and the campus groups at state schools to all the actual missionary-sending "boards." Your patrons can point you in the right direction. So can any short-term group you work with. And don't miss vital conferences like *Conquest* and *Urbana* that expose you to a world of opportunities (See "Stuff in the Back of the Book.")

You don't have to have all of this put together now. But making the connection means that as you move through junior high, high school, and college you pass these tests: *Are you getting good at reaching your peers? Does your home church believe in your gifts? Do the partners you meet think you would fit well on the mission field?*

Paddling Into the Sweet Part of the Wave

Waves always look bigger down the beach. The wave you miss always feels like the last killer ride of the day. And the job God assigns to someone else in his plan can look bigger and better than whatever he gives you to do.

But God made you unique for a reason—to serve him in a time and place where your gifts and talents change the world. Each of us, Paul says, is "God's workmanship, created in Christ Jesus to do good works, which God prepared in advance for us to do" (Ephesians 2:10). God wants you to find the place where *The Wave* is breaking just right. Like he's carved it just for you to catch and ride. Don't mistake that for a selfish "I'm going to do what feels good." It's a wise "I'm going to do what God made me to do." Catching *The Wave* won't always feel good. It's work. It's costly. But God wants you to find your place in his plan. It's where you can be one with *The Wave*.

Don't think that you can sit on the beach and wait for

God to whisper his will in your ear. You have to get out and try it. To catch *The Wave* now. Then God can show you how to catch it *then*. You have to catch *The Wave* here and there. Then God can show you how to catch it *everywhere*.

Let us fix our eyes on Jesus, the author

and perfecter of our faith, who for the

joy set before him endured the cross,

scorning its shame, and sat down at

the right hand of the throne of God.

—Hebrews 12:2

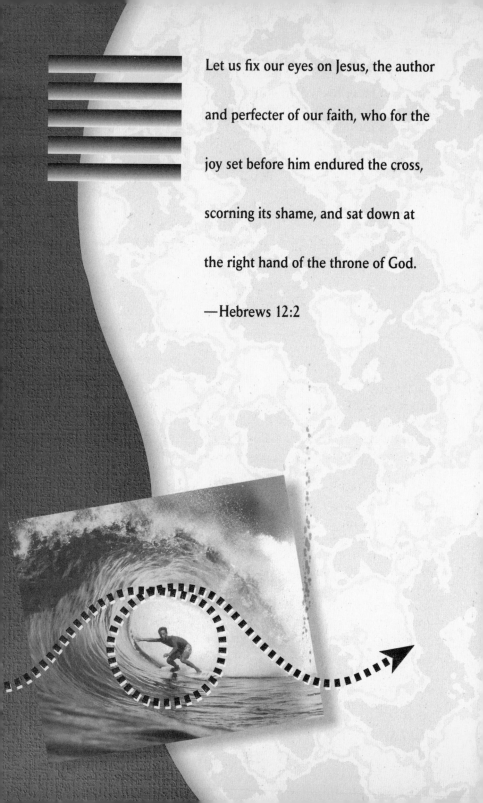

13

Riding *The Wave* Home

Mutiny was afoot as four members of First Church's summer work camp team huddled by themselves after breakfast. "This is a ripoff!" Janna whispered hysterically. "What were we thinking when we signed up for this trip? I can't believe I'm paying to work—and to sleep in a stinky, leaky tent!"

"You didn't pay very much," Ben shrugged. "What did you expect? Room service and mints on your pillow? My mom just wanted me out of the house for a couple weeks."

"They're being way too strict," Jon and Tom whined at the same time. Jon and Tom had both gone over the wall the night before—leaving the work site without permission—in search of mass quantities of Mountain Dew. When they were caught they argued that the cans in the vending machines on site were far too small to truly satisfy.

No one knows whether it was Ben, Janna, Jon, or Tom who started the tar fight later that morning. But at lunch all four of them showed up covered with black liquid gooze. Buckets of the stuff slimed the road they were supposed to be repairing. When their leaders sat the four down for a little chat about their attitudes and behavior, Janna exploded. "I

WANT TO GO HOME," she screeched. "YOU SAID THIS WOULD BE FUN!"

Riptides and Rocks

God isn't playing games. From before time began he planned to bring the world into existence so we could live in his love. He meant for us to have real relationships with himself and with each other—friendships where we would honor him as master and rely on his care, where we would love and serve him and each other. Even when the human race ran away from God he didn't abandon his plans. He sent Christ to die for our rebellion. He sent his Holy Spirit to pull us back to himself. And right now, all over the world, God is carrying out his goal of building a tight group of friends. That's *The Wave* crashing here, there, and everywhere.

God made you to be a WaveCatcher. He wired you for a special place in his world-changing plan. But there's something you need to know as you lunge into the surf. Being part of God's purpose is risky. When you try to catch *The Wave* you're likely to hit riptides and rocks. And maybe the biggest hazard you'll face is your own attitude.

———

Steve grew up in Hawaii. He can tick off sixteen reasons why surfing is stupid. His high school basketball coach convinced him, for starters, that if he went anywhere near the ocean he'd get bonked on the head by a board and never play ball again. And Steve assumed that if he surfed he couldn't be himself—he'd have to look, dress, walk, and talk exactly like every other surfer guy.

So Steve never hit the water—and liquid paradise bubbled away between his toes. He missed a once-in-a-lifetime opportunity. He's moved from Hawaii to the desert.

Rockheaded attitudes will keep you out of God's water:

Catching The Wave is for adults. Reaching the world isn't your job alone. It belongs to all Christians. Adults are supposed to lead the way. But Jesus was teaching in the temple

126

at age 12. While you're not Jesus, you're also no dirtball. You have his power working through you. You're capable of more than you think!

The job is too big. That's the whole point. It's infinitely big. Which makes it utterly important. And completely cool. Your task is to find your *piece* of the action.

I don't know what to do. Do not pass go. Do not collect $200. Go directly to chapter 6 and reread the no-brainer things God gave you to do.

I don't feel like it. Hmmm . . . pretty normal. Even Jesus didn't feel like dying on the cross. He did it anyway because he cared for you. When love acts, feelings follow.

I'm not sure what I believe. First law of carshopping: Beware of a Chevy saleperson who drives a Ford. In other words, you can't sell what you don't buy. But as you start to serve God and see God impact people, you'll find that catching *The Wave* can actually grow your faith. God is bigger than your shortcomings.

I have my whole life ahead of me. A few years ago Ryan was herded straight from high school to the mission field. Some days he did great. More often he was greeted with a *bah ha ha!* from people in a culture where age and education and experience were respected. You *do* have things to do and places to go and people to see. Don't shortchange your training. Don't shortcut your growing up. But don't settle in to a self-centered life where you ignore God. *Look for your place in his plan daily.*

I can think of better things to do. Or *It's not for me.* Or *I'm too busy with other stuff.* Ahhh . . . that's a big one. Whatever the words, it means the same thing: catching *The Wave* doesn't exactly buzz your funmeter.

Well, that all depends on how you define fun.

The Knee-High Surfer Guy

Nehemiah (*nee-uh-MY-uh*) was a guy in the Bible who dared to do what God put in front of him. Not that it was easy. But he managed to stick to God's plan—to not get tossed and eat sand.

Here's how it went. Back before Christ—in the *Foundation Stage* of the Bible—God had given his people the land of Israel as their home, a place where he would rule them as their kind King. But during the *Festering Stage* God's people little by little turned from God. In the end he allowed them to be conquered by the Persians and to be dragged from their land and forced to live in far-off Babylon. Their sacred city of Jerusalem was leveled—temple, fortified walls, everything. Decades later a few people returned to Jerusalem and rebuilt the temple. But the stone walls of the city were still broken down.

Onto the scene pops Nehemiah. He saw beyond his own comfort. He saw in his head what the walls could do. In everything he kept his mind on what needed to be done to do God's good will. Four pointers to pick up on how he pulled it off:

1. *Nehemiah knew about a need*. The destruction of Jerusalem was a physical sign of the people's distance from God. The lack of walls showed their weakness and vulnerability to attack. Not good: "When I heard these things," Nehemiah said, "I sat down and wept" (Nehemiah 1:4). He peeled his eyes off his own situation and looked hard at the plight of people a world away.

Things haven't gotten any better for the human race. People here, there, and everywhere live far from God. You reside on a pain-filled planet where five billion people don't know God, where a billion people have never even heard the name of Jesus. That's the need you've heard about for this whole book. That's the need you see whenever you take a short-term mission trip or look hard at your school. The point? You have to see the world the way God sees it.

2. *Nehemiah acted on the need*. Nehemiah didn't just hear and do nothing. He prayed (1:4–11). He decided to do what he could to rebuild the wall. He went to the king of Persia and got a royal heap of help (2:5–8). Nehemiah had the honored and trusted job of keeping bad guys from dropping rat poison in the king's cup. He left his cushy palace job to travel to a wasteland to pile up stones.

You don't have to wait for God to pound on your door

to tell you to go try to meet the needs you see. Jesus spoke the Great Commandment—that loving God and loving others are your first job. He pronounced the Great Commission—that you're to go and make disciples. And he included you in the Great Prediction—that you can spread God's News everywhere. So? You can get to work now.

3. *Nehemiah battled hard to meet the need*. Nehemiah's plan to rebuild the wall to protect the inhabitants of Jerusalem sounded like a great idea. Yet Nehemiah faced *ridicule* (4:1–3). His enemies said his wall was a joke. He faced *distraction* (6:2). His enemies tried to get him to quit his work and leave them in control. And he faced *fear* (6:5–6). His enemies threatened to spread rumors that would make the king of Persia halt the work. Nehemiah fought ridicule with prayer (4:4–6). He battled against distraction with focus and determination (6:3). He squashed fear with truth (6:8).

You might face *ridicule*: "You're no good at anything." "You're stupid to be a Christian." "What you're doing is a waste of time." You might face *distraction*: "Let's go do something else." "This is boring." "I've got better things to do." And you might face *fear*: "If you talk about Christ everyone will think you're a dork." "You'll flunk if the teacher hears you're a Christian." You can expect to face opposition. Fight it.

4. *Nehemiah succeeded in filling the need*. Nehemiah rallied people from Jerusalem and beyond to build the wall (6:15). Listen to what happened when they finished: "When all our enemies heard about this," Nehemiah said, "all the surrounding nations were afraid and lost their self-confidence, because they realized that this work had been done with the help of our God" (6:16). The wall protected the people from attack. It demonstrated God's care for his people.

When you catch *The Wave* you'll be sticking close to God, doing what God is doing. You'll show the world your awesome God. You'll affect the permanent destiny of people all around you—life overcoming death, light shining into darkness, heaven winning over hell. It's your chance to change the world.

A Different Kind of Fun

Nehemiah worked because he saw what was on the far side of his sweat. It's the same thing Jesus knew: "for the joy set before him" Jesus "endured the cross, scorning its shame, and sat down at the right hand of the throne of God" (Hebrews 12:2). Jesus saw the cross. He understood its pain. But he saw joy on the other side. He endured death so he could rise to save us.

You know what's on the far side of whatever tough stuff you go through to spread God's News. It's the tight group of friends God meant from the beginning. It's living in a perfect place with God and his people forever:

> And I heard a loud voice from the throne saying, "Now the dwelling of God is with men, and he will live with them. They will be his people, and God himself will be with them and be their God. He will wipe every tear from their eyes. There will be no more death or mourning or crying or pain, for the old order of things has passed away."
>
> Revelation 21:3–4

Catching *The Wave* is a different kind of fun.
It's for you. But it's also for *others*.
It's for now. But it's even more for *later*.
It's for *keeps*. It's a lifedream that lasts forever.
Believe it?
Then *Catch The Wave!*

Stuff in the Back of the Book

You want to *go*. You want to take God's Good News to people who don't know him. But how do you get there?

Start with people, places, and organizations you know. Most youth pastors, churches, parachurch groups like Youth for Christ or Young Life, denominations, and Christian schools can fill you in on opportunities to serve—for a summer, during spring break, or on Thanksgiving or Christmas vacation. They probably know of places around the corner and on the far side of the planet.

The Web site www.thewave.org/surfscoo.htm will also give you some leads. It focuses on opportunities available to junior and senior highers, highlighting just a *few* surfing schools—groups that can get you from here to there. Some organizations take groups—like a bunch of students from your church, along with adult leaders. Others sign up individuals and build teams of students drawn from all over. Most groups need college and adult volunteers to make their projects happen.

And here's even more stuff to help you catch *The Wave*:

Surfing Seminars:
Ways to learn about your world

Urbana–Student Missions Convention

What: Every three years the Urbana® student missions

convention draws more than 17,000 students to the campus of the University of Illinois at Urbana-Champaign for learning, worship, prayer, and discussion about missions and evangelism. Sponsored by InterVarsity Christian Fellowship, Urbana is a key place to explore short-term and career opportunities in missions for your college years and beyond. The next conference is December 2000.

Who: High school seniors and up.
Where: Urbana Promotion
P.O. Box 7895
Madison, WI 53707–7895
(608) 274–7995
http://www.gospelcom.net/iv

Surfspots:
Surfing the Web

You can't beat the Internet for up-to-the-minute info on taking God's News to the world. For starters, check out these gathering places, which do directories and links to the Web sites of many Christian organizations:

www.goshen.net
www.xc.org
www.gospelnet.com

Besides cruising through Web sites, you can get free, current news zapped right to your e-mail address. *Brigada* keeps you up to speed with a weekly mission update letter. Send an email to **brigada-today-subscribe@egroups.com** to subscribe—no subject or message is necessary—and you'll be signed up after you confirm your desire to receive Brigada. *Global Glimpse* widens your eyes with weekly key Good News breakthroughs from around the world—you can send a message to **jhanna@cproject.com** to sign up. Don't hog this information for yourself—it's meant for you to share with your youth group and your church!

Beach Equipment:
Stuff you'll want to know, read, watch, and do

Operation World by Patrick Johnstone. Over 600 pages of facts about your world—a great way to know how to pray (Zondervan Publishing House, 1993).

Run With the Vision by Bob Sjogren and Bill & Amy Stearns. The book to get if you're serious about being a missionary (Bethany House Publishers, 1995).

The Great Commission Handbook by Berry Publishing Services. A yearly magazine of places to go and things to do in missions (Berry Publishing Services is at 701 Main Street, Evanston, IL 60202, or call 708/869–1573).

The Compassion Project from Compassion International. Music, videos, and cool lessons available for your youth group to teach you about the world-crushing problem of poverty. Both Compassion and World Vision (below) give you the chance to sponsor children overseas. (Compassion International, P.O. BOX 7000, Colorado Springs, CO 80933; 800/336–7538)

30-Hour Famine from World Vision. A life-changing event that teaches you and your youth group about hunger, starvation, and disease—and helps raise money for those who suffer these problems. Great stuff. (World Vision, 34834 Weyerhaeuser Way South, Federal Way, WA 98001; 800/7-FAMINE)

Create in Me a Youth Ministry by Ridge Burns with Pam Campbell (Victor Books, 1986). Information about Sidewalk Sunday Schools.

ACMC. Provides materials and conferences to help churches catch *The Wave.* P.O. Box 3929, Peachtree City, GA 30269–7929; 770/631–9900.

National Network of Youth Ministries. Organizers of *See You At The Pole.* 17150 Via Del Campo, Suite 102, San Diego, CA 92127; 619/451–1111.

AD 2000 & Beyond Movement (and *Joshua Project 2000*). Mondo information and prayer materials about unreached peoples. 2860 S. Circle Drive, Suite 2112, Colorado Springs, CO 80906; 719/576–2000.

So You're Heading Home From a Short-term Missions Trip

Tens of thousand of teens take part in short-term missions trips each year. Maybe you're one of them. A huge purpose of *Catch the Wave!* is to help you take your trip home. Whether you're still serving, winging your way home, or back with familiar faces and places, reading *Catch the Wave!* will help you think through your experience.

The huge purpose of this note is to share with you seven tips to make your trip stick. Let's start with a tell-all question: How did being part of a missions project impact you? Whether you can't wait to get home or can't wait to go again, grab a sheet of paper and write a list of what you gained:

- Maybe you saw people living in poverty—and you feel grateful for all that God has given you.
- Maybe you spun dizzy with joy as you made friends with people in a different culture—and you wonder

how you'll ever see them again.

- ☞ Maybe you ditched bad habits and turned into a less-selfish person—and you're wondering how you'll stand strong.
- ☞ Maybe you grew to be best friends with your teammates—and you don't know how you'll stay close.
- ☞ And maybe you grabbed hold of God in a big way—and you're wishing you could feel that close to God all the time.

Going home from a missions trip is time to figure out what you gained—and brainstorm how you can keep growing.

God doesn't want your trip to be wasted. You don't want to lose what you listed—all those things you've learned. *Catch the Wave!* can't tell you *everything* you need to know to grow. But it's a great start. And before you dive into the book, here are those seven ways to hang on to what you have:

1. *Tell your story.* Not everyone will understand your experience. Some people think all missionaries are pushy. Other people have been on outreach trips—they might tell you all about theirs and not give an ear about yours. Others will want to know everything.

However people react, keep talking about Jesus. Whether you built a house, painted walls, or verbally told people about Jesus, what you experienced was real. And in some way you helped people hear, receive, and follow Jesus. That's cool!

2. *Don't settle for normal.* The world didn't stop turning while you were away. If your friends were a nasty influence before you left for your missions project, they'll probably be worse when you return. If your parents always seemed to be down on you, chances are that won't change overnight. Decide to be the new person you are—and finish this note for ways to find support to stay strong.

3. *Grab hold of your schedule. Catch the Wave!* is packed with ideas for serving "here, there, and everywhere," both now and later. If you learned that service is cool, carve it into your weekly calendar. Make it a habit to help people. You

may not be a cross-cultural, over-the-seas missionary, but you're still a full-time Christian. And when you serve, you put yourself in a place where God can continue to grow you.

4. *Get up and go on.* You want to be different. You'll never do it perfectly. God's forgiveness picks you up when you've failed. Circumstances will pound you, but God didn't create you to be a victim. He calls his children "more than conquerors." Think and pray about how you're going to apply the lessons you learned from your project *now*. And know that God will help you keep moving toward those goals.

5. *Win the battle for your brain.* Doing good isn't just about good feelings. "The Wave" you want to catch is this: *The Wave is God's plan to build a tight group of friends who belong to him—friends who honor him as their master and rely on his care now and forever.* You can be part of God's gargantuan plan to change the world, and as you read *Catch the Wave!* you'll find the Bible basis for making missions and service a permanent part of your life.

6. *Hang close to Christian friends.* People who think they're spiritual islands sink beneath the sea when hurricanes hit—or even when the constant lap of the ocean wears away their shore. You need Christian friends, even if going on a mission trip makes you feel way more spiritually mature than the people who stayed back home. (By the way, going on a missions trip doesn't make you automatically godly any more than going to McDonald's makes you a hamburger. So learn what you can from every believer around you.)

7. *Expect God to show up.* Count on God to teach you through the daily stuff of life—like struggles with school, friends, and family. God is active all over the world, and that includes your hometown. Short-term missions trips are a spiritual sprint. Whatever life God has mapped out for you is your real race—and it's a marathon. When you live close to God, he'll keep you moving. Being at home is part of God's plan to grow you spiritually and use you to change the world.

Whatever your experience, all of us who had a part of putting *Catch the Wave!* in your hands hope you will answer

Jesus' call to reach the world with the hope only he can provide. People everywhere need Jesus. We're rooting for you as you seek to change the world one corner at a time. *Catch the Wave!*

Acknowledgments

Catch the Wave! belongs to many people and organizations. Each of you poured into me things that spill out in the book. Thanks to:

Teen Missions International and the leaders and members of Venuzuela 1980, especially Lorne and Nora. Without all of you there would be no book.

John and Diana Sanny. For grabbing my feet and grounding them in God's Word.

Okontoe Mission Outreach and the ADC team. For a wild summer. And for my wife!

Peter and Kay Yang and Truth Lutheran Church of Taipei, Taiwan. For welcoming me not just once but twice. We'll be back. *Wǒ de jūng gwo hwà syàndzài jēn bù hǎu.*

YWAM of Taiwan. For a spot on the floor and many bowls of rice.

Dick Lee. For inviting us to the Chinese Evangelical Free Church of Monterey Park, California. Let's meet at The Dumpling Master. Or Fong Burgers. Or Grizzle Bowl, for that matter.

Fuller Theological Seminary. For teaching me to *think* about God's plan.

Students and leaders of Crossroads Youth Ministry at Elmbrook Church, especially all the King's Kids, Teen Helpers, Crossroads Choir, RadioHeads, and WorkCampers. You proved that serving Jesus was normal.

The students of Elmbrook and Mission Hills Church

who speak in this book. You are all wise beyond your years.

Daniel Hahn and Kim Sells. For being, like, gnarly WaveCatchers.

Stuart and Jill Briscoe and Val Hayworth. For fanning the flame of missions at Elmbrook and beyond.

Steve and Karen Lied, Tim and Jan Ryder, and Steve and Heather Godfrey. For your faithfulness.

Gayle "Widder" Will, Elizabeth Little, Bob Sjogren, John Hanna, Doug Lucas and team, and Mark Kelly. For putting me and thousands of others in touch with what God is doing here, there, and everywhere.

Steve Laube. Surfing's loss.

Bill and Amy Stearns. Without you there would also be no book. Thanks for the idea and for saying, "No, YOU get to write the book." Great mobilizers, Batman! You were the God-ordained push I needed to spill my heart on paper. I bequeath all twelve of my gray hairs to you.

Todd, Sally, Stefan, Elise, and Julianna. For your friendship and example. You give us more than we could ever give you.

Our parents—Roy and Lois Johnson and Tom and Pat Benson—and our families. Thanks to dad and mom for letting your baby go.

Everyone at Bethany House Publishers. Too much fun is being had by all. And Terry Dugan—for another great cover.

Finally, as always, to Nate, Karin, and Elise, for helping daddy write, and to Lyn, for walking God's will hand in hand with me for fifteen years. What patience! See you in Grand Marais.

Carpe Undam!
Kevin Walter Johnson